REVIEWS

"Anyone who wishes to pursue their bachelor's degree, focus on the courses within their major, and maximize their prior Judaic and life education and experience, should read this book. It will prove to be invaluable, for them and their parents. Mr. Frankel is to be commended for his research, presentation and overall contribution to our community."

RABBI PESACH LERNER, D.Adm.
Executive Vice President, National Council of Young Israel

"*The Bochur's Guide to College*" is written from and to the Jewish community interested in obtaining secular credentials for learning while at the same time honoring and sustaining the ethical and intellectual tradition rooted in study of the Torah. "*The Bochur's Guide*" is a knowledgeable overview of nontraditional education and educational opportunities for the Jewish community. Written with both young men and women in mind, the Guide features an appealingly casual, conversational tone that bridges Judaic cultural concepts with the language of nontraditional education... the goal is to provide its readers with the ability to direct them to achieve academic credentials in various ways, including never setting foot on a college campus or engaging in the discourse of the secular classroom. Nontraditional education is especially appropriate because this community has at its intellectual foundation the study of the Torah and other sacred writings."

DANA OFFERMAN, Ph.D.
Provost & Chief Academic Officer, Excelsior College
DAVID L. ELLIOTT, Ph.D.
Associate Dean, School of Liberal Arts, Excelsior College

"A beautifully organized guide to off-campus study that, for many, will prove indispensable."

RABBI HILLEL GOLDBERG
Executive Editor, Intermountain Jewish News

"When one embarks on a nontraditional route to a college degree, there is a bewildering array of options. Having a collection of academically sound opportunities in one volume of work, with guidance on navigating these new waters for the best fit with one's schedule and educational goals, is certain to minimize frustration and motivate enrollments, the very goals we have worked toward for more than thirty years. This book is a very worthwhile endeavor."

SHEILA A. MORRONI

Director, New York State Board of Regents, National Program on Noncollegiate Sponsored Instruction

"This is an excellent little guide as well as that very rare thing, a good idea. For... any student who needs some help understanding and navigating the U.S. nontraditional higher education system, this book is a blessing. Rabbi Frankel's style is informal and funny, and you can see that he has been there, done that, and done his homework as well."

MARYANNE LEGROW, Ph.D.

Assessment Coordinator, Charter Oak State College

"... Frankel has done an excellent job of explaining how to earn a college degree... You have done a wonderful job of fairly representing the colleges and accreditation. You have clearly demonstrated that you can think outside of the box and you challenge the students to do the same as they develop and execute their educational plans. *The Bochur's Guide* is a "must" read for students thinking of earning a college degree."

SHIRLEY M. ADAMS, Ph.D.

Provost, Charter Oak State College

"I recommend this publication to students interested in earning credit for the work they have done at a religious institution and applying it toward a secular degree. *Bochur* will help students understand the value of a degree and can help make the degree process understandable and a degree attainable. *Bochur* is full of meaningful information; and yet, it's easy to read and often humorous."

Dr. MERLE W. HARRIS

President Emerita, Charter Oak State College

The Bochur's Guide to College is admirable because it is everything that it claims to be. In a single smooth-reading volume, Rabbi Frankel has managed to produce a work which walks first-timers through every step of the program, pausing to insert very useful information and resources along the way. Every young man and woman who endeavors to pursue a college degree that will compliment his or her background in Judaics should read this book cover to cover.

Without hesitation we can knowledgeably endorse this book because our son and one of our daughters completed the AHS program in conjunction with Charter Oak State College. Both went on to receive their masters degrees, as they were well-prepared for that next step.

Rabbi Frankel had not yet published this invaluable resource, yet we had the benefit of walking through each step of the process with Rabbi Frankel's personal guidance. Reading *The Bochur's Guide to College* is like listening to Rabbi Frankel talking. His self-assuredness and relaxed tone which compliment his delivery of serious information come through in his writing style just as they do in person.

We have repeatedly referred young people who are college-bound to Rabbi Frankel for his expertise and guidance. Now we can conveniently hand a copy of *The Bochur's Guide to College* to interested students with the confidence that this introduction will lead to a fulfilling degree program guided by Rabbi Frankel.

ELIEZER and **MIRYAM VILINSKY**
Educational Support Services, Inc.
Monsey, NY

The Bochur's Guide to College

The Bochur's Guide to College

The Authoritative Guide to Da'as College

Reuven Frankel

Forshay Press
PO BOX 940
Tallman, NY 10982
(845) 510-3162
www.ForshayPress.com

ISBN: 978-0-9821978-2-0 (hb)
ISBN: 978-0-9821978-3-7 (pb)

Printed in the United States of America

to my mother

ADVICE

**This guide is not for parents.
This is not a warning but rather a word to the wise;
after all, sometimes ignorance is bliss.**

Please do not read this guide during davening, *leining,* **even** *bein gavra l'gavra,* **or during** *seder.*

About the Title

What's in a name? The working title for this book was *The Bochur's Guide to College: The Authoritative Guide to Da'as College.* However, it was never meant just for *bochurim* or men, it was just what I thought would be a catchy title and not one that would necessarily exclude female readers. In fact, my idea was to have a whole *shtikle* Torah in the beginning of the book to explain that this book is also geared for women, and then launch into a *halachic* discourse on *"lo silbash,"* discussing the prohibition of men acting or adopting the manner of women and vice versa, explaining and assuring the reader that no such prohibition of *"lo silbash"* would apply to women reading a book entitled *"The Bochur's Guide to College."* However, a colleague at one non-traditional college emailed me and suggested that, through my title, I may unintentionally limit my readership. She went on to relate the following, "The title is interesting and reminds me of a family story. In 1977, we went to Israel for our son's Bar Mitzvah. Our daughter was 10 and had very short hair. She did not take the ticket from the bus driver and the driver kept calling *"yeled!"* Of course, she kept going. She knew she was a *yaldah*. I hope the women will not have the same reaction to the book title." Well, I hope so too, since the title stuck...for now.

TABLE OF CONTENTS

ACKNOWLEDGEMENTS

A special thank you to my academic colleagues at Charter Oak State College. Dr. **Merle Harris**, President Emeritus, for taking the time to review and comment on the manuscript. Dr. **Shirley Adams**, Provost, who was kind enough to read and comment on the drafts. Her continuous commitment to the students' interest at Charter Oak may be unknown to most students but I can attest to that commitment. Thank you Dr. **Maryanne LeGrow**, for taking time to review the manuscript, and more importantly, for the years of friendship and spirited discussions of the finer points of nontraditional education.

I was fortunate to also receive input from members of the staff and administration of Excelsior College. Thank you Dr. **Dana Offerman**, Provost and Chief Academic Officer, and Dr. **David Elliott**, Associate Dean of the School of Liberal Arts, for reviewing and commenting on the manuscript. Thank you **Rachel Stolicky**, Academic Advisor, School of Liberal Arts, for reviewing sections of the manuscript.

Thank you Rabbi **Pesach Lerner** and Rabbi **Hillel Goldberg** for reviewing and commenting on the manuscript.

To my editor, Mrs. **Esther Deutsch**, who edited and reedited as sections were written, changed and added, thank you for keeping up. I would be remiss if I didn't mention her trusty foil and managing agent, her husband Moishe, who I am proud to call my friend.

To my students at AHS Institute and others who took the time to share their experiences with you the reader.

Thank you, **Adina** at Flamingo Design, for working with me to create a great layout and cover. My cartoonist, **Bob** at Millennium Design, really helped translate ideas and sketches into great drawings. Thanks to the **Hatbox** of Brooklyn for the hat featured on the cover.

To my **Rosh Hayeshiva** and **Sgan Rosh Yeshiva**, and their wives, who have opened their homes and hearts to me, and all their *talmidim*, and continuously teach, by example, what it means to live the Torah life.

To my parents, for their continuous love and dedication to me and my siblings. Always making us the center of their attention and encouraging each of us to excel in our own way. To my in-laws, who truly are a second set of parents.

Thank you to the One Above for giving me the opportunity to help others and for my partner in life, my wife **Devora**, who is always at my side and willing to lend a helping hand and offer her sound advice and ideas.

Reuven Frankel

May 2009

Section 1

INTRODUCTION

Earning your degree
shouldn't be as difficult as splitting the sea.

INTRODUCTION

Welcome

Welcome to the *Bochur's Guide to College*. The purpose of this book is to introduce you to nontraditional degree programs. By nontraditional, I refer to the ability to earn a college degree without the need to attend a traditional college campus. You will be introduced to colleges that give students the opportunity to earn a degree without ever stepping foot on their respective campuses. These are legitimate colleges, which hold regional accreditation and are recognized throughout the United States and abroad. However, unlike the traditional campus-based schools, these schools do not require students to come to campus. In recent years, even traditional colleges have begun offering full degree programs off-campus, through a variety of means of instruction, including correspondence study and online courses.

A Little Distance Learning History

In the book of Koheles we are taught *"there is nothing new under the sun,"* and this applies to distance learning or non-traditional education too. Distance education is not just some new fad brought about by the internet, although it is true that in the last ten years or so it seems that is what everyone is talking about. People think, *"Wow, now with the internet I don't have to go to campus to attend a college course. I can do it right from the computer."* However, distance education is far from something new. In 1883, an ad in a Swedish newspaper offered the opportunity to study *"composition through the medium of the post."* We find that study by mail existed back in England in 1840, when Isaac Pitman offered shorthand instruction via the English penny post. In 1883, Chautauqua College of Liberal Arts was authorized by New York State to grant degrees to students who completed summer workshops and correspondence study. That was only slightly before the internet boom. In 1953, the University of Wisconsin had 10,000 active students enrolled in correspondence study courses.

Enter Technology

As technology developed, distance education spread from print to courses over the radio. In 1925, the State University of Iowa offered five courses for credit over the airwaves. With the invention of the television, it too was used to broadcast courses. In the 1960's, the University of Wisconsin offered continuing education courses to physicians via audio-conferencing. Later this was adapted by some colleges for college courses as well.

Jumping across the pond, in 1969, the British Open University was established as a degree granting institution. Over 180,000 students currently study at OU.

Then came the internet, and everyone heard about distance education. Unfortunately, a lot of the publicity was negative. While diploma mills existed before the internet, finding one, and perhaps even starting one, was more difficult. With the internet came the proliferation of diploma mills and all of those wonderful spam messages offering you a degree for only a certain amount of money, and in only a matter of days. The truth is that there are plenty of legitimate and quality nontraditional degree programs out there, and this guide is here to help you through the process.

This Book

This book is here to serve as a guide, to hold your hand as you research and plan your educational goals. As we describe the nuts and bolts of a college education, the pieces eventually fit together to form a college degree. Just this week, a student called in confusion, explaining that until recently she thought she understood the college degree process. However, after learning of all the options and opportunities that exist to earn college credit, she became overwhelmed and frustrated. In response, I described the degree process as a jigsaw puzzle; all the pieces have to come together to make up a college degree. The completed puzzle represents the degree, and it is our job to fit the correct pieces into the correct places in order to complete the puzzle. However, unlike a jigsaw puzzle, where each piece has its own place and only one piece fits into any given place, a college degree offers several alternates for each piece. For example, if you need to take a history course you might not be limited to a specific history course; you might have a choice of different history courses, any of which would fit into the gap you are looking to fill. It is my hope that this book will be your friend and mentor as you learn about and plan for your college degree.

Why Choose Nontraditional Education?

While the purpose of this guide is not to discuss the merit (or lack thereof) of earning a college degree, there are several tidbits that we will share. People pursue degrees for a variety of reasons: some for personal satisfaction, others for promotions, and some feel they need it to get their foot in the door. In going through the help-wanted sections of the newspaper, you may notice that even the most mundane of jobs lists a college degree as a requirement for employment. The College Board's *"Education Pays 2007"* report discusses the value of a college degree. The report indicates that on average, in 2005, a worker with a high school diploma earns $31,500, while a worker with a bachelor's degree earns $50,900. This is a significant difference.

So why choose a nontraditional college degree? For some, flexibility in terms of schedule is important. Not everyone can stop what they're doing, rearrange their schedule, and attend traditional campus-based courses. For others, and this may be true for most of you, it is about the ability to take control of your educational studies, the ability to choose your surroundings and to avoid situations that run counter to Torah values and traditions. The way I see it, there are three major benefits of the nontraditional degree.

TIME: The nontraditional degree offers students flexibility in terms of how and when to study. In addition, the student can often complete a degree more quickly than by taking traditional college courses.

FOCUS: The nontraditional degree allows you to focus primarily on what matters most in life. For many, it's the opportunity to focus on Jewish studies, and the nontraditional degree may allow students to maximize their time spent in yeshiva and apply that knowledge toward earning the degree.

COST: In many cases, the expenses of the nontraditional degree may be far less than that of a traditional campus-based degree. In terms of costs, a recent report, *"Trends in College Pricing"* breaks down the average cost of attending college. Public four-year schools cost $6,185; public four-year schools, for out-of-state students, cost $16,640; private nonprofit colleges cost $23,172; public two-year institutions cost $2361; and for-profit schools cost $12,089. All of these costs are per year, and are not costs for the whole degree. Many students find that they can earn a nontraditional degree for under $10,000. This is a significant savings.

A Word of Caution

Approximately thirteen years ago I had the opportunity to attend a *shiur* early Shavous morning given by a noted Rav and *Posek*. The *shiur*'s title was *"College: Assur, Mutar or Mitzva."* Suffice it to say that the attendees were captivated despite the early hour of 3:00AM. The conclusion of the *shiur* surprised most, I believe, as the Rav concluded, that attending college may at some times be *assur*, at some times *mutar*, and even, at times, a *mitzvah*. The issue of college has been discussed by many *rabbonim* and *poskim* and you should discuss it with yours. The opportunity to earn a degree off-campus or via distance learning may alleviate some concerns, while the flexibility in selecting what courses to take in order to satisfy the degree requirements at some of the nontraditional colleges discussed in this book may allay some concerns as well.

The Bottom Line

All in all, earning a college degree is a serious and time-consuming endeavor. This book is here to help walk you through the process. All the seriousness can be overwhelming at times, which is why I have attempted to make reading this guide fun and enjoyable. I hope you'll agree that it is.

Section 2

OVERVIEW

"Puzzled?"

OVERVIEW

This guide is written specifically for you, the yeshiva or Bais Yaakov student or graduate. So, you want to go about earning a degree but have no idea how. Well, that's why we put this book together—to give you and your parents an idea of what is behind that elusive and much sought after college degree.

Where to begin...hmmm? Let us start at the beginning. An undergraduate college degree comes in two common sizes, the associate's and the bachelor's. The associate's is generally two years in duration or sixty credits, while the bachelor's or baccalaureate is a four year degree or 120 credits. When speaking about undergraduate degrees, most people are referring to the bachelor's, as the associate's is used only as a stepping stone to the bachelor's by many.

For the most part, we'll be discussing the bachelor's degree. Thus, when we refer to a degree throughout this work, we will be referring to the bachelor's, unless otherwise noted.

Okay, we have 120 credits that we have to earn. Most college courses are three credit courses, so one will generally take forty or so courses to earn one's degree. Great, you

Why earn a degree? The reasons are many and they range from personal satisfaction (some people actually enjoy learning new things), to professional reasons (people need credentials to get the job they seek or to reach a new pay grade), but the most common reason might just be because your parents are making you do it.

We start right away speaking about a degree. But what in fact is a degree? The degree is more than a mere cheftza; it is more than just a paper with printed words. It is a siman that the person it is awarded to successfully completed a specified course of study. However, the question remains: Did he just go through the motions as a mere bystander? Or did he in fact retain the information studied and was able to apply it to new scenarios.

Many, correctly or incorrectly, view the undergraduate degree as a means to an end, as a form of hishtadlus *to get their foot into the door of a business or professional position or as a ticket into graduate school where they study in the field of their interest.*

Notice that we mention that the associate's or bachelor's degrees are generally understood as a course of study lasting two or four years. Of course any self respecting ben *or* bas *Torah understands that is only for everyone else, and would expect to earn or at least get their degree in a matter of weeks or months. This guide is for those of us who fall somewhere between the two extremes.*

say, let's start. But wait a minute. You cannot just take any combination of 40 courses or 120 credits and expect to earn a degree. Not so fast! You see, colleges want you to have a certain breadth and depth of coursework in a variety of areas. This is called the distribution requirement. What this basically means is that you, the student, have to demonstrate knowledge in specific areas; your courses have to be distributed among several defined areas. Generally speaking, the degree is split into three broad areas. These are: 1. general education, 2. the major, focus or concentration, and 3. (general) electives. Don't worry, we'll discuss each of these areas one by one.

General Education: As its name implies, this area requires the student to demonstrate knowledge in an assortment of areas of study that the colleges feel that every graduate should have knowledge of. The basics include English composition, Mathematics, Science, History and others, depending on the college. The general education component of the degree will generally consist of a quarter or third of the degree, or thirty or so credits.

Next up is the **Area of Concentration**, or the **Major**. This is where you demonstrate knowledge in a specific field or discipline.

Some common ones are Business Administration or Education. While these may seem to be very specific areas, colleges also have majors or concentrations in Humanities or Liberal Studies. These concentrations allow the student to utilize a wide variety of different courses to satisfy the requirements.

Now we come to the **Electives**. Here you can run wild with your courses. Explore new disciplines or areas of interest. The electives area allows for the most flexibility, as you can use almost any courses to satisfy the requirements.

Each undergraduate degree also has a minimum number of liberal arts or arts and sciences credits that must be applied toward the degree. Courses will generally fall within three categories: humanities, social sciences and history, and natural sciences and mathematics. A sample listing of courses or disciplines that will fall under each of these categories is listed in the appendix. Courses which do not fall into the liberal arts or arts and sciences category are generally classified as applied professional credits.

Another term you should be familiar with is "upper level credits". The upper level designation is assigned to advanced or intensive courses which are not introductory.

Ah, the general education component. Why, oh why do we need one? This part of the degree elicits the most confusion from the bochurim. Why, they ask, do I need science history or even English if I am interested in accounting or business? I don't plan to become a doctor, so why do I need science? Well, the college is looking to produce velts mentchen, **people who are well-rounded, and no, there is no physical connotation meant.**

With the concentration or major we finally get to tachlis. **Some people actually have a plan of what they want to do and how they plan to pursue their desired profession or job. Say you are interested in accounting. The major or concentration is the area where much of this course work will fall in to place. Enough talk about those** *yichidim who may actually have a detailed plan of action. What about the rest of the olam? The good news is you don't really need too much of a plan, as many colleges allow you to create what's called a liberal arts major or concentration, and this allows you to feel out your interests and put together a very eclectic group of courses.*

Forty courses?! You've got to be kidding. Don't worry, we know you don't really want to sit through forty courses in a classroom, and this is why you're reading this guide and why we actually wrote it. Believe it or not, we didn't just write this guide to give a running commentary on the subject in these margins.

Traditionally, "low" or "lower level" credits are all offered during the freshman and sophomore years (within the first two years of college), and "upper level" credits generally refers to courses taken at the junior or senior level, or the third and fourth year of college. At the associate degree level, all the credits may be lower level. There are no upper level requirements. However, on the bachelor degree level there will be upper level requirements, and the minimum number of upper level credits that must be applied toward the degree will vary from college to college.

Now that you have a basic idea of the areas of distribution, we will give some examples using the degree requirements from several different colleges later on in "The Colleges" section of this guide.

Now that I know what components a degree is made up of, how in the world do I go about satisfying the requirements? Where do I take these courses? And do I really have to sit in class or take forty courses? Well... I'm glad you asked. There are several ways to earn credits, from the traditional classroom to online courses and a whole lot in between. The most common way to earn credit is by sitting in the classroom for a college course, of course. If you're reading this book, traditional campus based education is likely not for you. Many of you, however, will take some courses on a college campus and you should know that, depending on the college, there may be morning, afternoon or night classes available. This will allow you to fit the courses around your work or Yeshiva schedules.

Online

Many colleges now offer online courses. What exactly constitutes an online course will vary from college to college and even from instructor to instructor within a given college or university. The degree of student-to-instructor interaction or even student-to-student interaction will also vary greatly. Some require you to log on to an online classroom for a minimum amount of time during the week. Course requirements may include posting to online discussions, assignments, papers and exams. Some require proctored exams, while others offer online examinations from the comfort of your local computer lab or home. Many online courses still require the use of textbooks.

Correspondence

Correspondence, the original form of distance learning, is still very much alive and well at some colleges. However, the number of institutions offering print-based courses

Online. Yes, the triefena internet and we don't say this lightly; there is a lot of garbage out there on the virtual information superhighway and one should speak it over with a Rebbe or Rav before embarking on this highway.

Good old-fashioned correspondence courses are also known to many as home study courses. With

the advent of technology, especially the internet, this mode of study is quickly disappearing. However, there are still colleges offering courses by traditional correspondence as they still wish to serve underprivileged, rural communities and the prison population, and we get to jump on the bandwagon too. Not, chas v'sholom, *the prison bandwagon, of course.*

is quickly dwindling as they move to web-based courses. Students registering for correspondence courses will generally receive a syllabus. Sometime this consists of course notes or a course study guide, and students will be required to purchase a textbook and complete the series of written assignments followed by an examination. The number of examinations required will vary from course to course, and some colleges may also require the student to find a proctor to administer the exam. In many cases, students will be able to submit their assignments or contact their instructor via mail, fax, or e-mail. All this, of course, depends on the course and the college.

Credit by Exam

In addition to taking traditional college courses or distance learning courses, students can also earn credit through testing. Later on in this guide, we will provide you with an overview of some of the more popular testing programs along with those which we feel are most appropriate. Two of the most popular testing programs are the CLEP and AP (Advanced Placement) programs. Many of you may be familiar with these. Several Yeshivas offer AP courses, which culminate with the AP exam, in high school. The most popular credit by exam program is CLEP, or College Level Examination Program. We will take a closer look at the testing process, examination programs and available exams later on.

The Colleges

So now we have a little knowledge of the components that make up a degree, but where do we get the degree from? This guide was written for students who want to earn a college degree primarily through nontraditional methods, and we had some specific colleges in mind. The colleges had to meet several criteria, namely accreditation and flexibility in terms of accepting credits earned through nontraditional means, such as credit-by-exam, distance learning and portfolio assessment. In this guide we highlight two colleges: Charter Oak State College and Excelsior College.

Section 3

TESTING

Advanced Placement/AP

College Level Examination Program/CLEP

Dantes/DSST

Excelsior College Exams/ECE

Thomas Edison State College Examination Program/TECEP

New York University Language Exams

Graduate Records Exams/GRE

Ohio University Course Credit by Exam

EVERYTHING I NEED TO KNOW I LEARNED IN CHEDER

CREDIT BY EXAMINATION

Credit by examination is a great way to earn college credit both quickly and inexpensively. Quickly, because you are not constrained by the traditional semester course structure and class time requirements. Traditionally, the average three credit college course consists of forty-five hours of class time and additional homework time, which can include up to ninety hours of homework. The theory behind the credit by exam model is that what you know is more important than how it is learned. So if you can demonstrate that you know what the average student attending a comparable traditional college course of the same subject would know, then you deserve the credit too. Another plus of the credit by exam format is the cost. The costs of the exams are generally significantly less than a comparable college course.

Many exams may also be taken by high school students. This is a great way to, so to speak, kill two birds with one stone. If you feel up to it academically, make a list of courses you are currently taking in high school and compare it to the list of exams available for credit. If you find some that match up, take a look at the outline of topics covered on the exam and see what you may

The faher. Don't let the sound of it scare you away. The exam process is very manageable. Testing is a gevaldig way to earn college credit. It's really great if you already have knowledge in the exam's subject area. For example, if you have been doing bookkeeping or accounting for a business, you may already have all the knowledge needed to pass an exam in accounting.

Even if you have no knowledge in the subject area of the exam, you can still prepare on your own to take the exam. Basically, you make a leining on the material; most exam programs provide an outline of topics on a given exam as well as a list of suggested texts.

be covering in class, noting which topics are not covered and setting a study plan in place. Take your knowledge of the required topics to the next level by using one of the suggested textbooks or find a college study guide for the course. Test yourself on the material and see how well you are doing.

When it came to writing about preparing for credit by examination, I had a dilemma: should I include the test preparation materials produced by commercial publishers? The organizations that administer or create exams offer outlines showing the topics covered on the exam, a list of suggested readings as well as sample questions. Some of this material is free, and some of it is available online or in book form for a nominal fee. In addition to this *"official test preparation material,"* there is also test preparation materials produced by commercial publishers in either print form or online. Initially, I was hesitant to discuss or include information on these commercial publishers. However, I noticed that this option was discussed in a student newsletter produced by one of the colleges mentioned elsewhere in this guide. So while yes, there are commercially available test preparation materials, which many feel can help the students to prepare for the examinations, I wish to also offer a disclaimer as found in

How you decide to study for the exam is up to you. Some people use the recommended texts and study beiyun; others take a more bekius approach.

the Excelsior college catalogs and website. Excelsior publishes the following word of caution:

> "There are tutorial firms, test preparation services, and for-profit publishing companies that sell materials with the claim that their materials will help students prepare for and pass Excelsior College Examinations. The College is not affiliated with any test preparation company and does not endorse the products or services of any test preparation organization...Using the services of a test preparation provider is up to individual students and whether or not they believe they need these services. We do not review the materials any company produces for content."

While this disclaimer specifically addresses test prep for the Excelsior College Examinations, the words of caution can be applied to other testing programs as well.

This section will highlight some of the available testing programs that are available to students. Many of these exams are available to high school-age students as well. Throughout this section we have also included some of the experiences that students have shared regarding their degrees and testing odysseys.

This section does not discuss the Judaic Studies exam programs that may be available. Some Judaic exam programs are administered by organizations or institutions mentioned in the Community Programs section. Throughout this section you will also find AHS Institute Judaic courses or exams mentioned by students. Many students interviewed have taken AHS courses or exams, however, this is by no means the only option.

Meet Sara

I chose to pursue a degree through distance learning for three main reasons.

1) *it enabled me to pursue my degree in a kosher setting.*
2) *it offered me the flexibility to work part time.*
3) *it offered great portability, as I did not know where I would end up living.*

I found distance learning very fulfilling and came out knowing the information. I was happy not to have to sit through long lectures that sometimes have a tendency to go off on tangents. With distance learning I was able to focus on the learning at hand. I especially liked the "human element" in my distance learning courses in speech-language pathology from Longwood University and the Judaic courses from AHS Institute. Unlike just taking standardized exams for credit, I had the option of calling or emailing an instructor with my questions or need for clarification on some course reading.

I definitely recommend distance learning to motivated individuals who are ready to think for themselves.

Sara graduated with a B.S. from Excelsior College, with credits from a number of sources. She earned credit for her year in seminary through the TI study abroad program, CLEP, AP, AHS Institute, and summer courses at Maalot Baltimore. She also completed her speech-language pathology master's pre-requisite coursework online, and is currently pursuing a Master's in Speech-Language Pathology online through Nova University.

CLEP PROGRAM

The largest testing program is the College Level Examination Program or CLEP. The exams offered are lower level exams, based on courses generally studied during the first two years of college. There are two groups of exams: the general and subject exams.

Your first source of information as to what is on the exams, as well as some suggested study aids, is the Official CLEP Guide published by the College Board. You can find this book at Barnes and Noble, Amazon and even at the library. This guide includes an outline of topics found on each exam, some sample exam questions, and a suggested reading list.

The exams are now computer based, and all the answers are entered via the keyboard. Exams are ninety minutes in length and are generally multiple choice questions; some exams have fill-in questions, and the English Composition has a second section with an essay component.

The cost is under $100 per exam.

More information on CLEP can be found at **www.collegeboard.org** or by calling 800-257-9558.

You should note the copyright year on the book, as the list of exams offered does change, as does the format or content. So while you may be able to find a great deal on a five year old CLEP Guide, be sure to try and compare it with a more recent edition. With the money you save you can give some more tzedaka and have in mind for some Divine help with your exam.

The CLEP Guide reading list is generally made up of college text books on the subject. However, if you are like most bochurim who already know everything and do not wish to read the text book cover to cover, you might want to take advantage of a study guide on the topic matter—just to brush up, of course—instead of reading the textbook.

CLEP PROGRAM

Composition and Literature

American Literature

Analyzing and Interpreting Literature

English Composition

English Literature

Freshman College Composition

Humanities

Foreign Languages

French Language (Levels 1 and 2)

German Language (Levels 1 and 2)

Spanish Language (Levels 1 and 2)

History and Social Sciences

American Government

Human Growth and Development

Introduction to Educational Psychology

Introductory Psychology

Introductory Sociology

Principles of Macroeconomics

Principles of Microeconomics

Social Sciences and History

U.S. History I: Early Colonization to 1877

U.S. History II: 1865 to the Present

Western Civilization I: Ancient Near East to 1648

Western Civilization II: 1648 to the Present

CLEP PROGRAM

Science and Mathematics

Biology

Calculus

Chemistry

College Algebra

College Mathematics

Natural Sciences

Pre-calculus

Business

Financial Accounting

Introductory Business Law

Information Systems and Computer Applications

Principles of Management

Principles of Marketing

Some CLEPs have an optional essay section. Be sure to check with the college you plan to earn your degree from and see if the essay section is required to earn credit. The most common example I've come across is the English Composition CLEP. Charter Oak and Excelsior require the English Composition with Essay in order to award credit.

Additionally, it is important to note that while Excelsior College will grant credit for the CLEP English Composition with Essay exam, it will not satisfy their English Writing Requirement. However, the Excelsior English Composition Exam will satisfy the writing requirement.

Meet Malka

I chose to pursue a degree via distance learning as it allowed me to work full time while in school. Furthermore, I found that I enjoy working independently and being able to set the pace of my studies.

I earned my degree primarily through Empire State College online courses, some exams, and a course at AHS Institute.

Just a helpful bit of info…I discovered that Empire will recognize the Psychology GRE for quite a number of credits. I took the Psych GRE and scored 600 (about average). Empire sent me a letter stating that according to their evaluations, that would be the equivalent of 8 lower level credits and 12 upper level credits. To study for the Psych GRE I used the test guides put out by Kaplan, Princeton Review, etc. If you know the guides and have common sense, you know most of the test. It's kind of like a CLEP, just more material.

Malka is a member of the Empire State College graduating class of 2008. She enrolled in the College's Center for Distance Learning where she took the bulk of her courses online. She also took two independent study courses from Empire in Jewish history, which she designed and studied together with her mentor. Malka was recently accepted to the Psy.D. (doctorate in clinical psychology) program at a major New Jersey university.

AP PROGRAM

Advanced Placement Exams (AP®) are generally offered in participating high schools. Students can also prepare to take the exams by studying independently if their school does not participate and by contacting AP services at 888-225-5427. They will help put you in contact with local AP Coordinators.

I generally don't discuss this option with students unless they are in a school that offers AP courses and exams. If this is the case, you should take advantage of the program offered at your school.

The cost is under $100 per exam.

The AP program offers 37 courses spread across 22 subject areas.

> I took several CLEPs: Psychology, Sociology, Human Growth and Development, and College Mathematics. I started using the REA test preparation materials. However, I needed some tutoring for math because it was getting too complicated. I took all these CLEPs after I got back from seminary. I found that they were pretty easy after studying the REA material thoroughly.
>
> **C.H. Canada**

> I took the Chemistry College Math, Introductory Psychology, Introductory Sociology, U.S. History I, Biology and Analyzing and Interpreting Literature CLEP exams. Use the REA guides whenever available. I found that REA gives the best preparation. For the College Mathematics exam I used Kaplan's. I also took the Excelsior College Writing Exam. Excelsior College puts out an excellent spiral-bound study guide for this exam and is quite reasonable too.
>
> **Dina from Toronto**

AP PROGRAM

Art History

Biology

Calculus AB

Calculus BC

Chemistry

Chinese Language and Culture

Computer Science A

Computer Science AB Comp Government & Politics

Human Geography

Italian Language and Culture

Japanese Language and Culture

Latin Literature

Latin: Vergil

Music Theory

Physics B

Physics C

Psychology

Spanish Language

Spanish Literature

Statistics

Studio Art

U.S. Government & Politics

U.S. History

World History

Meet Chanie

I like to work at my own pace. If you're disciplined you may be able to speed up the learning process. I especially liked the idea of earning credit through examinations. I would rather read books and teach myself than sit through classes.

I chose to earn my degree through Excelsior College. My credits mainly came from three sources; online speech-language leveling courses (prerequisites) from University of Alaska, CLEP and DSST exams and AHS Institute Judaic courses and exams.

If you plan on earning credits through exams, try and find some people who took the exams you are looking into and find out what books and study aids they recommend.

Chanie earned her B.A. in Liberal Studies with a focus in Communication Disorders. She is currently completing her first year at the University of Kentucky online Master's in Speech-Language Pathology. The program is mostly online but does require a short residency at the University.

EXCELSIOR COLLEGE EXAMS

Excelsior College Exams are accepted at Excelsior College and hundreds of other colleges and universities around the world. Choose from over 50 exams in the arts and sciences, business, nursing, and education. Many exams offer upper-level credit. Students can study independently, using an array of valuable learning resources available directly from Excelsior College, and some exams have guided learning packages available from Excelsior College.

Exams can be taken at Pearson Professional Centers®, open up to six days a week. When you take a multiple choice exam, you will get an unofficial grade report on the spot.

To register for an exam, go to the Excelsior College website at **www.excelsior.edu** and click on the Exam link or call 888-72EXAMS to register by phone.

High school students are also welcome to take Excelsior College Exams. Exams are generally three or six credits each with the nursing exams being three, four, six or eight credits each. Most exams cost $235, and some are $335. Nursing exams are $270 each.

Excelsior College and Pearson VUE have partnered to offer a new credit-by-exam program called UExcel. For more information or to register, visit www.uexceltest.com or call Pearson VUE at 888-224-6383. Free exam content guides are available on the website.

As of May 2009 there are four exams available:
Calculus–4 credits
Physics–6 credits
Political Science–3 credits
Psychology–3 credits

College Writing and Statistics are coming soon.

EXCELSIOR COLLEGE EXAMS

Arts & Sciences

Abnormal Psychology

American Dream

Anatomy & Physiology

Bioethics: Philosophical Issues

Cultural Diversity

Earth Science

English Composition

Ethics: Theory & Practice

Foundations of Gerontology

Introduction to Music

Juvenile Delinquency

Life Span Developmental Psychology

Microbiology

Organizational Behavior

Pathophysiology

Psychology of Adulthood and Aging

Religions of the World

Research Methods in Psychology

Social Psychology

World Conflicts Since 1990

World Population

Business

Ethics: Theory & Practice

Human Resource Management

Labor Relations

Organizational Behavior

EXCELSIOR COLLEGE EXAMS

Education
Literacy Instruction in Elementary School

Nursing
Essentials of Nursing Care: Health Safety

Essentials of Nursing Care: Health Differences

Essentials of Nursing Care: Chronicity

Essentials of Nursing Care: Reproductive Health

Health Differences Across the Life Span 1

Health Differences Across the Life Span 2

Health Differences Across the Life Span 3

Nursing Concepts 1,2,3,4,5,6

Nursing Concepts: Foundations of Professional Practice

Transition to the Registered Professional Nurse Role

Fundamentals of Nursing

Maternal & Child Nursing (Associate)

Maternity Nursing

Community Focused Nursing

Management in Nursing

Research in Nursing

Adult Nursing

Maternal & Child Nursing (baccalaureate)

Psychiatric/Mental Health Nursing

Remember, Charter Oak State College, along with many other colleges, will award credit for Excelsior College Exams.

Meet Esther

I have moved from Lakewood to Israel and back during the course of my studies, and that is one reason why distance learning was good for me. I also liked the ability to work at my own pace. I earned credit from a number of sources. I took CLEPs, DSSTs, AHS Judaic courses and Jewish Subject Exams from TTI. Distance learning and testing worked best for me since it was cheaper and I was able to stay home with my son.

DL is not for everyone. Some people have an easier time going to school. You have to be motivated to study on your own and really do it. Some people feel more of a push going to a college and sitting in class. It's like the difference between having a treadmill at home or going to the gym :-).

Esther currently has approximately 85 credits and is planning on earning a B.A. in Psychology from Thomas Edison State College.

DSST EXAMS

The DSST (Dantes Subject Standardized Test) program also provides the opportunity for people to earn college credit for what they have learned outside of the traditional classroom. DSST exams are accepted at over 1,900 colleges and universities nationwide and 90,000 DSSTs are administered to individuals annually.

The DSST program enables people to use their knowledge acquired outside the classroom to accomplish their educational goals.

There are 37 exams to choose from in the areas of Social Science, Business, Mathematics, Applied Technology, Humanities, and Physical Science. More information can be obtained by calling 877-471-9860 or by visiting www.getcollegecredit.com. The website has available exam fact sheets as free downloads, as well as practice exams for a fee.

The fee per exam is under $100.

> I took only two CLEP exams—one was a math which I took at the end of 10th grade and was practically a final for what we had learned that year. I also took an English Comp CLEP which I found to be quite easy. I used one of their study books and did a few practice exams. I found them to be extremely helpful as they helped give me an idea as to the type of answers they were looking for. Once I did a few of the practice exams, I got a good feel for what types of questions they would ask. The actual exam consisted of different examples but practically the same questions.
>
> **Anonymous, Jerusalem, Israel**

DSST Exams

Mathematics

Fundamentals of College Algebra; 3B

Principles of Statistics; 3B

Social Science

Art of the Western World; 3B

Western Europe since 1945; 3B

An Introduction to the Modern Middle East; 3B

Human/Cultural Geography; 3B

Rise and Fall of the Soviet Union; 3BU

A History of the Vietnam War; 3B

The Civil War and Reconstruction; 3BU

Foundations of Education, 3B

Lifespan Developmental Psychology, 3B

General Anthropology; 3B

Drug and Alcohol Abuse; 3BU

Introduction to Law Enforcement; 3B

Criminal Justice; 3B

Fundamentals of Counseling; 3B

Business

Principles of Finance; 3BU

Principles of Financial Accounting; 3B

Human Resource Management; 3B

Organizational Behavior; 3B

Principles of Supervision; 3B

Business Law II; 3BU

Introduction to Computing; 3B

Introduction to Business; 3B

DSST Exams

Money and Banking; 3BU

Personal Finance; 3B

Management Information Systems; 3BU

Business Mathematics; 3B

Physical Science

Astronomy; 3B

Here's to Your Health; 3B

Environment and Humanity: The Race to Save the Planet; 3B

Principles of Physical Science I; 3B

Physical Geology; 3B

Applied Technology

Technical Writing; 3B

Humanities

Ethics in America; 3B

Introduction to World Religions; 3B

Principles of Public Speaking; 3B

Meet Moishe

As a yeshiva bachur with his mind set on getting into business school, I didn't care about what field my undergraduate degree would be in. A degree in liberal arts would be just fine, as it would only be a stepping stone to a master's degree in business.

I wasn't interested in sitting in a classroom for four years. I enrolled in Excelsior because I'm in a program in Brooklyn that works with Excelsior, called TTI (Testing and Training International). I took a bunch of CLEPs and a lot of Jewish Study exams through TTI, which worked out well because I knew the material before I took the test, so there was minimal studying involved. Loneliness isn't a problem, because I'm in Yeshiva. I started this whole process in 11th grade, and this my seventh year. Now that there's an end in sight, it's easy to stay motivated.

Moishe began the college process while still in mesivta by taking some CLEPs. His degree is taking longer than expected but graduation is in sight.

TECEP®

Thomas Edison State College offers a series of exams called TECEP®. These exams were designed for adult learners to allow them to earn college credits without taking formal courses. Information for these exams can be found on the Thomas Edison State College website at **www.tesc.edu**, or by calling the College at 888-442-8372. The website includes test descriptions, lists of topics covered, suggested study materials and sample questions. Please call or check the website for an updated list of available exams.

As of May 2009, the cost per credit is $80 for students enrolled in Thomas Edison and $160 for nonenrolled students. Exams are three credits each.

> Here are the exams I took: CLEP—Human Growth and Development and Math. DSST—Foundations of Education. Excelsior exams—Literacy Instruction in Elementary Schools and College Writing. NYU—Hebrew and Yiddish exams. I took the Biology CLEP while studying for the Regents exam. I passed the Regents with a 98% and failed the CLEP. I don't think it is enough to just study for the Regents. You also need to use the CLEP book.
>
> **Anonymous Jerusalem, Israel**

> I took many CLEPs, College Mathematics, Analyzing and Interpreting Literature, Human Growth and Development, Introductory Psychology, and Abnormal Psychology. I also took a college writing exam from Excelsior College. I actually took Race to Save the Planet, a DSST exam, but failed by two points. To study for these exams I generally went online and looked for some free study material. However, I recommend using study guides with sample test questions.
>
> **L.S. Baltimore, Maryland**

TECEP® Exams

English Composition

English Composition I (ENC-101-TE)

English Composition II (ENC-102-TE)

Humanities

The History of Western Art II (ART-167-TE)

Public Relations Thought and Practice (COM-210-TE)

Technical Writing (ENG-201-TE)

Introduction to the History of Film (FIL-160-TE)

Introduction to News Reporting (JOU-110-TE)

Shakespeare I (LIT-320-TE)

Introduction to the Art of Theater (THA-101-TE)

Social Sciences

Labor Relations and Collective Bargaining (LAS-321-TE)

Advanced Labor Relations and Collective Bargaining (LAS-322-TE)

Introduction to Political Science (POS-101-TE)

Introduction to Psychology (PSY-101-TE)

Developmental Psychology (PSY-211-TE)

Psychology of Women (PSY-270-TE)

Thanatology: An Understanding of Death and Dying (PSY-300-TE)

Research in Experimental Psychology (PSY-322-TE)

Introduction to Counseling (PSY-331-TE)

Behavior Modification Techniques in Counseling (PSY-339-TE)

Abnormal Psychology (PSY-350-TE)

Psychology of Personality (PSY-352-TE)

Organizational Behavior (PSY-361-TE)

Industrial Psychology (PSY-363-TE)

Introduction to Social Psychology (PSY-370-TE)

TECEP® Exams

Marriage and the Family (SOC-210-TE)

Social Gerontology (SOC-315-TE)

Alcohol Abuse: Fundamental Facts (SOS-301-TE)

Substance Abuse: Fundamental Facts (SOS-303-TE)

Natural Sciences/Mathematics

The Science of Nutrition (BIO-208-TE)

Anatomy and Physiology BIO-211/212 (BIO-211-TE)

QBASIC (COS-110-TE)

C Programming (COS-116-TE)

BASIC (COS-117-TE)

Operating Systems (COS-352-TE)

Physical Geology (GEO-151-TE)

Physics I (PHY-111-TE)

Physics II (PHY-112-TE)

Principles of Statistics (STA-201-TE)

Business and Management

Federal Income Taxation (ACC-421-TE)

Business in Society (BUS-311-TE)

Business Policy (BUS-421-TE)

Introduction to Computer Information Systems (CIS-102-TE)

Database Management (CIS-311-TE)

Principles of Finance (FIN-301-TE)

Security Analysis and Portfolio Management (FIN-321-TE)

Financial Institutions and Markets (FIN-331-TE)

International Finance (FIN-334-TE)

Business Law (LAW-201-TE)

Principles of Management (MAN-301-TE)

TECEP® EXAMS

Organizational Behavior (MAN-311-TE)

Labor Relations and Collective Bargaining (MAN-321-TE)

Advanced Labor Relations and Collective Bargaining (MAN-322-TE)

Human Resources Management (MAN-331-TE)

Introduction to Marketing (MAR-301-TE)

Marketing Communications (MAR-321-TE)

Sales Management (MAR-322-TE)

Advertising (MAR-323-TE)

Marketing Channels (MAR-331-TE)

Marketing Research (MAR-411-TE)

Marketing Management Strategy (MAR-425-TE)

Operations Management (OPM-301-TE)

Computer Applications

Word Processing Fundamentals (SES-131-TE)

Human Services

Counselor Training: Short-Term Client Systems (COU-322-TE)

Kinesiology (FIT-211-TE)

Community Health (HEA-301-TE)

Introduction to Human Services (HUS-101-TE)

TECEP exams are also accepted by Charter Oak State College and Excelsior College.

Meet Shoshana

I didn't want to go to college and have to be tied down to living in a certain location, and I chose Charter Oak State College. Charter Oak worked for me because it has flexible transfer policies and it allows students to earn an unlimited amount of credit by exam. I earned college credit through online courses, CLEP, DANTES, Excelsior exams and AHS Institute Judaic courses. It did feel a little lonely not being in an actual classroom, but it was great to be able to work at my own pace. The first year was tough because I worked alone, but during my second year, I had a friend who did some of the same courses as me, and studying together made things much easier.

I'm working toward a degree in nutrition, which Charter Oak does not grant. I am working on a B.S. in Individualized Studies from Charter Oak. I am earning my Masters in Nutrition from another university, so I needed to find which pre-requisites were necessary for acceptance there and include them in my Concentration Plan of Study for Charter Oak. You need to be very careful that every course and exam you take has accreditation that is recognized by the universities you've chosen for both your undergraduate and graduate degrees. My graduate university advised me to take an online course that is equivalent to one of its online pre-requisites, but that course wasn't recognized by Charter Oak. Being aware that different universities have different standards will save you time, money, and extra work. Also, be persistent! While some courses and exams are really easy, others take a lot more time and effort; just remember that it's all worth it in the end.

NYU LANGUAGE EXAMS

Proficiency testing is available for people wishing to measure their knowledge of a foreign language. The results of the test, which are transcripted by NYU, may be used by universities to grant academic credit or award advanced placement. Tests are given by appointment at NYU and may also be administered at off-site locations in the U.S. or abroad.

Exam fees for fall 2007 are $290 for 12-point (two-hour) exams; $390 for 16-point (three-hour) exams. There is an additional registration fee and off site fees.

For further information, to make an appointment, or to request a brochure, please call (212) 998-7030, or visit **www.scps.nyu.edu/trans**.

Approximately fifty language exams are offered. The ones of most interest to the readers of this guide are probably Hebrew and Yiddish.

The reaction from students is mixed when hearing suggestions that they take the NYU Hebrew exam. Some say, "Hey, I know Hebrew. That should be easy." Others have a very different reaction. "Hebrew? I don't speak Hebrew, I don't read modern Hebrew! How can I take the exam?" To those students we say: stop thinking about it like a Yeshiva guy or Bais Yaakov girl. View it from the college angle. Do you know the Aleph Beis? Can you read Hebrew? The average student stepping into a traditional college class in Hebrew may never have even seen aleph beis. Enough said.

Meet Tova

I started out attending a regular college, but I was really horrified at the effect it was having on me. I decided to switch to Excelsior because of that, and because I thought I could probably earn more credits each semester by cutting out travel time.

I also thought it would be more portable, allowing me to move anywhere at the drop of a hat with no problems. In addition to my Excelsior courses, I took CLEP and AP courses, as well as community college classes, classes in Maalot, and AHS courses. I also had credits from college classes I took in high school.

I had an excellent experience with credit by exam: they were the cheapest way to earn credits, and I definitely had to study and know the material, which I think is good. It's a little bit scary having an all or none exam rather than assignments and a final, but I would have done more, except that they're lower level credits only.

I did feel isolated, but I remedied that by taking classes at a local seminary. Otherwise I would've gone stir crazy; I'm able to work alone, but I'm a social person.

I stayed motivated mostly by dividing up my coursework and marking down the dates I needed to finish the work. I found this to be a very powerful motivator, even if it was self-imposed. Studying at the same time every day helped, as did enjoying the classes I took and being genuinely interested in the material.

Tova graduated from Excelsior College and is currently enrolled in an online Registered Dietician (RD) program at Eastern Michigan University.

GRE EXAMS

The GRE Subject exams are commonly used for students to demonstrate their knowledge in a specific field. These exams are used as part of the admissions process for entry into graduate programs. The important point for you, the nontraditional student, is that some colleges will actually award college credit for this exam toward their undergraduate degree programs. Excelsior College and Charter Oak State College will award up to 30 credits depending on the student's score.

There are eight exams to select from. The fee for each subject exam is $130. Exams are three hours in length and are offered three times a year, in paper and pencil format. Visit www.ets.org/gre/ or call 866-473-4373 for exam information. The website also has Subject Test Practice Books available as free downloads.

Biochemistry, Cell and Molecular Biology

Biology

Chemistry

Computer Science

Literature in English

Mathematics

Physics

Psychology

Many of you may have heard of the GRE or the Graduate Record Examinations. What you may not be aware of is the existence of GRE Subject Tests, which help measure a student's knowledge of a specific discipline.

Excelsior College grants between three and thirty credits per exam depending on your score.

Charter Oak State College grants up to eighteen or twenty-four credits depending on the exam.

Meet Daniel

I was in yeshiva and wanted to pursue a career in the dental profession. There was no college system set up with my yeshiva; however, AHS Institute came through and I was able to graduate from Charter Oak State College with Honors, while still maintaining my full time yeshiva schedule. I am currently in NYU College of Dentistry. I was very happy to get credit for sitting and learning what I wanted to be learning (Judaic Studies) and not other unnecessary secular courses. AHS was there every step of the way. Whenever I needed something done they were thorough and quick to respond and took care of anything I needed to further my degree. AHS has very reasonable prices per credit. My experience with AHS was awesome. I am quick to recommend them to anyone wanting to finish their degree fast without crazy costs and to someone who wants to spend minimal time in a secular environment... they really care about every individual's success. They were able to accommodate me while I was in Israel, Connecticut, New York, and California. Wherever I went they were just a phone call away. Thank you very much, AHS Institute and Charter Oak State College for helping me every step of the way towards my goal.

Daniel was one of several pre-med students that I have dealt with over the years. He combined exams, distance learning, AHS distance learning Judaic courses and traditional college courses to earn his degree from Charter Oak State College. In case you were wondering, he had to attend traditional college courses and labs for his science courses.

OHIO UNIVERSITY

Ohio University offers students a variety of distance learning opportunities. In addition to online and independent study courses some courses are available by what is called Course Credit by Examination (CCE). A wide variety of courses are available by examination. Essentially, the student registers for the exam, receives a syllabus which outlines the courses requirements, grading policy, and the textbook required. Some courses also include sample exam questions with the syllabus. The student has six months to prepare and take the exam. The grade on the exam is the grade for the course.

Lower level exams are open to high school students who have the recommendation of their principal or guidance counselor.

As of July 2007 exam fees are $69 per quarter credit hour.

For more information contact Ohio University at **www.ohio.edu** and click on the Distance Learning link. Or call the Life Long and Distance Learning office at 800-444-2910.

Students should keep in mind that Ohio University operates on the quarter hour system and not the semester hour system.

1.5 quarter hours =
1 semester hour

3.0 quarter hours =
2 semester hours

4.5 quarter hours =
3 semester hours

6.0 quarter hours =
4 semester hours

7.5 quarter hours =
5 semester hours

Meet Mimi

I would say there are 4 central reasons for why I chose to pursue a degree through nontraditional means.

1) *it allowed me to set my own pace. I did not want to spend 4 years earning my undergraduate degree.*
2) *it gave me flexibility to study and work on courses on my own time. I like to work on my schooling in the middle of the night.*
3) *it gave me the flexibility to work full time as I pursued my bachelor's degree.*
4) *it allowed me to control my environment. I did not want to be exposed to some of the culture that may be found on a traditional college campus.*

I used a number of methods to earn college credit. I took some CLEPs, Excelsior College Exams, the NYU Hebrew Language Exam, and independent study courses from Empire State College. Empire State also allowed me to earn college credit for some of my seminary studies through prior learning assessment. I was able to earn credit in Judaic studies and special education. Through prior learning assessment I also earned credit for first aid and CPR. I also took some the science courses that I needed at a local community college.

For the right student distance learning is a great option. Whichever nontraditional college a student chooses, I would recommend they sit down and talk it over with a friend who previously went through the program. I did this before enrolling in Empire State and found it very helpful.

Mimi graduated from Empire State College in June 2008 and is currently attending SUNY Downstate for a Masters in Occupational Therapy.

"OVERNIGHT SUCCESS"

what you know is more important than how you know it

Bears' Guide to Earning Degrees by Distance Learning writes, "*A National-al Guard sergeant we know of crammed for, took, and passed three GREs in a row, thereby earning 90 semester units in ten and a half hours of testing. Then he took five CLEP exams in two days and earned 30 more units, which was enough to earn an accredited Bachelor's degree, start to finish, in 18 hours, starting absolutely from scratch with no college credit. Not typical. Maybe not even advisable. But doable!*"

Is this possible? Probably. However, let's be honest: will the majority of you be able to pull it off? I think we would all agree that the answer is a resounding *"NO!"* Does this incident make the nontraditional degree any less legitimate? I don't believe so. Remember, the credo of many nontraditional colleges is **what you know** is more important than **how you know** it. Let's take a less extreme example of a student I personally know. She took a GRE Subject Test in Psychology and here is what she wrote: "*I took the Psych GRE and scored 600 (about average). Empire*

sent me a letter stating that according to their evaluations, that would be the equiv-alent of 8 lower level credits and 12 upper level credits. All studying for the Psych GRE involves is studying the test guides put out by Kaplan, Princeton Review, etc. If you know the guides and have common sense, you know most of the test. It's kind of like a CLEP, just a tad more material." On the one hand, we can take her experience at face value and say, "Wow, that sounds easy, a little review and I can sit for an exam and earn 20 credits." On the other hand, looking at her academic interest, one would learn that she has an interest in psychology and she took psychology courses. She insists that one can do well on the exam without ever having taken a psychology course. She later clarified, "*It's like studying for a CLEP, a difficult one, in a subject that you have no previous knowledge of.*" Perhaps the most impor-tant key to her success is that she enjoys the subject and enjoyed learning more about the exam topics from the various study guides she used. Here's another ex-ample using a CLEP exam. The American Government CLEP is a favorite example students who are up on current events to take a look at the topics found on the American Government exam. If you are an adult living in the U.S. it is very likely that you have picked up much of the knowledge covered on this exam. I ask if they are familiar with the three branches of government and their responsibilities. Are you familiar with the Constitution? Bill of Rights? We recently had a lot of coverage on the Supreme Court and the various positions of the appointees on some famous cases with the latest appointments of two new justices. The recent presidential election also brought much of the knowledge covered on this exam to the news headlines and everyday conversation.

Getting back to the Guardsman, it is likely that he brought a wealth of informal learning experiences and knowledge with him to the examination. So while it may be true that he earned enough credit for the degree over a twenty-hour period of testing, this accounts for the time his knowledge of the subject areas was assessed. It does not, however, account for the time and effort it took to gain that knowledge.

A special thank you to Todd Siben, Thomas Edison State College Senior Program Advisor, Liberal Arts and Sciences Programs, who inspired the title for this section and on whose experience this cartoon is based.

Remember, what you know is more important than how you know it.

Section 4

CORRESPONDENCE STUDY

❦

Indiana University
Louisiana State University
Ohio University
Portland State University
Sam Houston State University
Texas Tech University
University of Idaho
University of Florida
University of Missouri
University of North Dakota
University of Wyoming

CORRESPONDENCE COURSES

Some students do not have access to the internet or try to limit their time online, in which case print-based courses may be a great option for learning and earning college credit. However, with the advent of technology, more and more colleges and universities are moving from print-based to online courses. Some schools are expanding their course offering to include online courses, while others are entirely replacing print-based courses with online courses.

Correspondence courses generally involve, at least, a study guide prepared by the college or the instructor, and require the student to purchase a textbook. The course study guide varies by institution and instructor. The study guide may just consist of a simple syllabus, instructions for the course, and a list of assignments, or may also include notes from the instructor that help clarify the course readings, and sample exams or self-check quizzes that you can use to test yourself. Generally speaking, correspondence courses require the student to take one or more proctored exams. At times, print-based courses may require audio or visual material, such as recorded lectures or documentary type videos to enhance and reinforce the learning process.

What is a correspondence course?
Traditionally, it has referred to print-based courses offered by mail. Now some schools use the term for both print-based and online courses.

CORRESPONDENCE STUDY IS ALSO REFERRED TO AS INDEPENDENT STUDY BY SOME INSTITUTIONS.

As with some credit by examination programs, these schools may allow high school students to enroll in select college correspondence courses. Some require high school students to submit a letter of recommendation from a school principal or guidance counselor.

Highlighted in this section are several regionally accredited colleges and universities offering print-based courses. Some of these schools also offer courses online. Additionally, several of these schools also offer degree programs that can be completed at a distance.

Keep in mind that correspondence courses require lots of motivation. For some students the flexibility of a correspondence course is a blessing, for others it is a disaster. There are no classes to attend, and if you don't set aside time to study you may find yourself at the course deadline without ever have gotten started. Some courses allow up to nine months or a year for completion, and that gives students a lot of opportunity to make excuses and to procrastinate. Some programs offer extensions, but often this just gives students more time to drag their feet. The bottom line is, set yourself a realistic goal, make a schedule, and stick to it.

The information in this section is quoted and adapted from the respective college or university website or publications.

INDIANA UNIVERSITY

The School of Continuing Studies was established in 1975 and is one of the largest distance education providers in the United States. The School of Continuing Studies offers more than 195 undergraduate courses through its Independent Study Program. You complete the same amount of work and receive the same credit as you would in similar on-campus courses. Courses are offered online and by correspondence.

Through its General Studies Degree Program, the School of Continuing Studies also offers two Indiana University degrees at a distance: the Associate of Arts in General Studies (60 credit hours) and the Bachelor of General Studies (120 credit hours). Distance students complete their degree by taking undergraduate courses through the Independent Study Program. It is now possible to earn both the associate and bachelor's degree by taking only online courses.

Tuition for non-Indiana residents is $197.06 per credit plus fees.

Indiana University
School of Continuing Studies
790 E. Kirkwood Avenue
Bloomington, Indiana 47405-7101
800-334-1011
812-855-2292
Fax 812-855-8680
scs@indiana.edu
http://scs.indiana.edu

LOUISIANA STATE UNIVERSITY

Educating students at a distance has been part of LSU's mission for over 80 years. When University Extension was formed in 1924, Correspondence Study was one of two original departments. The department name was changed to the Office of Independent Study in 1982 to emphasize the self-paced nature of the courses. At LSU Independent & Distance Learning (IDL), you can live your life while you work toward your dreams. Independent learning courses allow you to achieve your educational goals while you maintain other important work, home, and community commitments.

Whether you want to earn college credit to apply toward a degree, to enhance your professional credentials, or to expand your horizons, LSU IDL offers the courses and flexibility you need to reach your goal.

Tuition is $250 per three credit course. Students have up to nine months to complete their course.

LSU Independent & Distance Learning
1225 Pleasant Hall
Louisiana State University
Baton Rouge, LA 70803
800-234-5046
225-578-3171
Fax: 225-578-3090
iservices@outreach.lsu.edu
http://www.is.lsu.edu

LSU offers a nice selection of print-based courses at a very reasonable tuition rate.

OHIO UNIVERSITY

In addition to the Ohio University Credit by Exam program discussed in the Testing section, the university also offers correspondence courses. Independent and Distance Learning correspondence courses provide a highly structured method of independent study involving a tutorial relationship with a faculty member who guides your learning and monitors your progress. The detailed study guide, prepared by your instructor, provides an overview and the lesson units that direct you through the course. The textbook and other print materials are often supplemented with audio or videotapes. You may enroll any time during the year, and you have eight months to complete a course.

Most lessons require you to submit answers to objective questions or write brief essays or both. Some lessons may require a paper or project. The study guide often includes self-check tests that let you monitor your own progress. Generally, two supervised examinations are required—a midcourse and a final examination.

To enroll in correspondence courses it is not necessary for you to have a high school diploma if you are an adult. High school students recommended by their principal or guidance counselor are eligible to enroll in lower-division courses.

Current tuition is $136 per quarter credit hour.

Haning Hall
Ohio University
Athens, Ohio 45701
800-444-2910
www.ohiou.edu/independent

PORTLAND STATE UNIVERSITY

Independent Study courses are self-paced non-term-based correspondence courses using either print-based or online course guides. You can begin a course any day of the year (except holidays) and work directly with the instructor to complete the required coursework within one to 12 months (with the option of a six-month extension).

$101 per university credit regardless of location of residence.

Portland State University
Independent Study
PO Box 1491
Portland, OR 97207-14911
503-725-4865
800-547-8887 ext 4865
fax: 503-725-4880
http://www.istudy.pdx.edu/

SAM HOUSTON STATE UNIVERSITY

Through the Correspondence Course Division, Sam Houston State University provides the opportunity for qualified individuals to obtain college credit through correspondence course study. Students may study at their own rate and at the time and place of their choosing. Students have a maximum of 12 months from the date of enrollment to complete a correspondence course. A correspondence course may not be completed in less than 60 days from the date of enrollment.

A 3 credit course is $240.00; $70 per credit and a $30 administrative fee per course.

Sam Houston State University
Correspondence Course Division
Box 2536
Sam Houston State University
Huntsville, Texas 77341-2536
936.294.3909
cor_sav@shsu.edu
www.shsu/edu/~cor_www/

TEXAS TECH UNIVERSITY

Texas Tech University's Division of Outreach & Distance Education (ODE) offers correspondence courses (print-based and online) for college credit. Academically strong high school students may choose to take a dual-credit course, allowing them to earn both high school and college credit simultaneously. Students have six months from the date of enrollment to complete an ODE course, including the final examination.

ODE's flexible college offerings include independent study courses and a Bachelor of General Studies degree (B.G.S.). Many currently enrolled students choose to earn credit that can be applied toward their degree plans, while others, who may be unable to attend college due to personal or professional obligations, can earn a degree from home.

Tuition and fees are the same for Texas residents and non-residents. Current tuition for college level courses is approximately $150 per credit plus fees.

Texas Tech University
Outreach & Distance Education
9th & Indiana Ave
Lubbock, TX 79409-2191
800.692.6877
806.742.7200
http://www.depts.ttu.edu/ode/

UNIVERSITY OF IDAHO

Independent Study in Idaho (ISI) offers distance college education courses in online and print-based formats. ISI courses are designed to help students pace themselves in their learning. The flexible program allows students to enroll at any time and from any place. Students have up to a year to complete their course.

Tuition is $100 per credit and a $25 administrative fee per course. Independent Study in Idaho was created in 1973 by the Idaho State Board of Education as a cooperative of four accredited Idaho institutions led by the University of Idaho. Other cooperating members include Boise State University, Idaho State University, and Lewis-Clark State College. Each member institution is accredited by the Northwest Commission on Colleges and Universities (NWCCU), the region's accrediting agency. Idaho residency is not required. Students may register for ISI courses without applying for admission to the ISI cooperating institutions.

Independent Study in Idaho
University of Idaho
PO Box 443225
Moscow ID 83844-3225
(877) 464-3246
(208) 885-6641
Fax: (208) 885-5738
indepst@uidaho.edu
www.uidaho.edu/isi

UNIVERSITY OF FLORIDA

The Division of Continuing Education (DCE) Flexible Learning courses are distance courses with some available online, some print-based, and some are in both formats. Flexible Learning is "flexible" in that anyone can enroll at any time. Students have 32 weeks to complete their course. Courses cannot be completed in less than 8 weeks.

Students do not have to be enrolled at UF to register for one or more courses. High school students enrolling in college credit courses must have written permission from their counselor, principal, or parent to enroll.

Current tuition is $112.41, per credit, for Florida residents and $135.61 for non-residents. Each course has a $90 administration fee.

University of Florida
2209 NW 13th St., Suite D
Gainesville FL 32609
352- 392-1711
800-327-4218
fax: (352) 392-6950
learn@dce.ufl.edu
http://www.correspondencestudy.ufl.edu/

UNIVERSITY OF MISSOURI

The University of Missouri's Center for Distance and Independent Study offers more than 150 distance learning courses. You may choose independent study courses in 35 subject areas. Approximately 5,000 students enroll in our university courses every year. Print-based and online courses are available. Students have nine months to complete a course. Courses may also be available to high school students.

The Center also offers students the opportunity to finish a bachelor's degree from wherever you are. The Bachelor of General Studies Degree allows students to complete a degree online.

Current tuition is $245.60 per credit plus administrative fees.

University of Missouri
Center for Distance and Independent Study
136 Clark Hall
Columbia, MO 65211-4200
800-609-3727
573-882-2491
cdis@missouri.edu
http://cdis.missouri.edu

By the end of 2009 the University of Missouri plans to convert their print-based courses to an online format. The courses will still be self-paced but available only online.

UNIVERSITY OF NORTH DAKOTA

The University of North Dakota has a long history in correspondence study, offering courses since 1910. More than 2,500 people enroll in courses offered through UND's Correspondence & Online Studies program each year. Students have up to 9 months to complete a course.

Correspondence & Online Studies offers two types of courses: open enrollment courses and semester-based courses. In open-enrollment courses, you may choose from more than 90 undergraduate courses for academic credit in a variety of subjects from accounting to the arts. Courses are offered by traditional mail and online. You can register by mail or online. Semester-based courses are offered online, vary from semester to semester, and follow the University's academic calendar. They are offered in an independent study format, so you can work on your course(s) at anytime and from anywhere. Federal financial aid may be used for these courses.

Tuition is currently $219.84 per credit.

Department of Correspondence & Online Studies
Division of Continuing Education
University of North Dakota
Gustafson Hall Room 103
3264 Campus Road Stop 9021
Grand Forks, ND 58202-9021
(701) 777-2661
(800) 342-8230
correspondence@mail.und.nodak.edu
https://www.conted.und.edu/correspondence/

University of Wyoming

The University of Wyoming was the first university west of the Missouri to offer correspondence courses. Correspondence study from the University of Wyoming provides the opportunity to earn college-level course credit without attending regularly scheduled on-campus classes. Students can enroll in a course at any time, and the nine-month enrollment period allows students to complete coursework at their own pace. It is not necessary to be admitted to the university to enroll in a correspondence study course at UW.

The course syllabus directs you step-by-step through the coursework and assigns written work for each unit of study. You prepare each written assignment and submit it to correspondence study along with any questions you have for your instructor. The instructor then corrects and grades your lesson, answers your questions, makes suggestions, and returns your work.

Tuition is approximately $100 per credit.

University of Wyoming
Outreach Credit Programs
Dept. 3274
1000 E. University Ave.
340 Wyo Hall
Laramie, WY 82071
800-448-7801
uwcorr@uwyo.edu
http://outreach.uwyo.edu/correspondence/

Section 5

ONLINE COURSES

❧

Charter Oak Online Courses
Excelsior Online Courses

I'LL BE RIGHT DOWN FOR DINNER, MOM...
I'M STILL IN SCHOOL!

ONLINE COURSES

Online courses can generally be accessed any time and anywhere you have an internet connection. Online courses vary in the way they make use of the web for either presentation of material or communication. Some schools or instructors use the web in lieu of sending students print-based materials. For example, an online course may consist of the same materials described in the previous section discussing correspondence courses, and the "online" component of the course may simply be a posting of the syllabus and a list of required assignments. Basically, instead of receiving a packet of information in the mail, an "online" version of the course may simply require you to go to the web and read the information from your screen or print it off the web.

Yet another version of an online course would be adapting a print-based version of a course and harnessing some of the technology offered by computers and the internet. These courses may include audio or video lectures, links to additional learning materials on the internet, the ability to submit required assignments online, and self-scoring practice quizzes.

Until now, we discussed online courses as

Online courses provide what can be termed a "virtual classroom," giving students some of the advantages of the traditional classroom by way of interacting with a teacher as well as fellow students. Again, for the most part, the interaction will be solely asynchronous, allowing you to "attend" class on your own time. Additionally, the term- or semester- based online courses offers students greater structure than self-paced courses, providing a more structured timeline for the student who may tend to procrastinate.

close cousins to traditional, print-based, and student-paced correspondence courses. However, many schools offer online semester or term-based courses. Unlike the traditional self-paced correspondence courses, these courses are conducted in "virtual classrooms," requiring assignments to be submitted on a set schedule and involving student-to-student interaction via "threaded discussions." Interaction is asynchronous, meaning that students interact by posting comments any time during their allotted schedule. Some online courses also have a chat room to allow students to interact in real time or synchronously. These online courses still provide the student with great flexibility, as the student still chooses when and where to log in to participate in the discussions and to submit assignments, as long as he or she logs in during the times noted on the course schedule outlined in the syllabus. Additionally, many online courses do not require proctored exams, and all student work and submissions are handled online.

Online courses vary in format. So do your research and make sure the course is right for your schedule and learning style. Charter Oak State College and Excelsior College are two of many schools that offer semester or term based online courses.

Charter Oak Online Courses

Charter Oak State College offers online courses on a 15-week schedule. Five week and eight week accelerated courses are also offered. Students interested in registering for online courses should go to the College's website and read about the online courses offered.

Charter Oak online courses require students to submit their assignments in a timely fashion. Courses also include a "threaded discussion" where students post comments during the week. For the most part, the courses are asynchronous and do not require students to be online at a specific time. However, some courses have team projects that require students to "meet" online at a mutually decided time. As far as testing goes, many online courses and all of the accelerated courses have required testing built into the course and do not require you to find a proctor. Some courses assign a final paper or project instead of conducting exams.

> Charter Oak has an online tutorial for students new to online learning, an online student orientation, free tutoring, online library, and a help desk for technical assistance.

EXCELSIOR ONLINE COURSES

Excelsior College offers most of their online courses on a 15-week term schedule, with courses starting every other month. The Excelsior website gives prospective students the opportunity to view a multimedia demonstration of a sample course. Additional pertinent information on online courses can be found in their publication, Undergraduate Courses Helpful Information, under the publications link.

Excelsior online courses provide students with course accesses from anywhere there is an internet connection. The course platform provides access to the syllabus, readings, notes, gradebook and discussion boards. Textbooks and other course materials may still need to be purchased. Examinations are generally not proctored.

> Excelsior College also offers CD-ROM courses. Similar to online courses, CD-ROM courses are term-based and require a computer. However, these courses do not require the student to access the internet. Assignments can be submitted via email, standard mail, or fax.

Section 6

OTHER SOURCES OF CREDIT

⚜

Yeshiva Credits

Yeshiva Credits & Excelsior College

Study Abroad

Noncollegiate Courses and Exams

Prior Learning Assessment

OTHER SOURCES OF CREDITS

In this section we take a look at some other methods of earning college credit besides for the standard testing programs. We won't discuss the traditional method of attending a regular college course; instead, we discuss other non-traditional options.

First we'll briefly explore "Yeshiva Credits." Yeshiva credits are vastly misunderstood and we hope to set the record straight on the matter. Next we explore an extension of the yeshiva credit issue, credits earned in yeshiva or seminary in Eretz Yisroel.

We will then briefly touch upon what are called noncollegiate learning programs, which exist in the secular and Jewish world, in yeshivas and the world of business. Under this category we will also learn about the testing options in the field of Judaic studies.

And finally, we introduce the concept of college credit for life experience.

YESHIVA CREDITS

What are yeshiva credits? Loosely defined, yeshiva credits are those credits earned for courses taken in yeshiva. Some yeshivas are accredited; others are not. The yeshivas that are accredited are generally accredited by AARTS, the Association of Advanced Rabbinical and Talmudic Schools. There are some regionally accredited colleges that will accept these yeshiva credits in transfer toward an undergraduate degree. Some require that they be from an AARTS accredited institution; others do not. In terms of the colleges discussed in this book, Excelsior will grant 30 credits in transfer if a student has earned at least 45 credits at an AARTS accredited institution. Some schools recognize a yeshiva degree as meeting their requirement of an undergraduate degree for admission to a graduate program. For information on yeshiva studies while in Israel please see the next section "Study Abroad."

YESHIVA CREDITS & EXCELSIOR COLLEGE

Any student who presents an official transcript stating that he completed a minimum of 45 credits, with at least a GPA of 2.0, from an Association of Advanced Rabbinical and Talmudic Schools (AARTS) accredited school will receive 30 lower-level credits in transfer as follows:

Hebrew (Talmudic)	6
Yiddish (Talmudic)	3
Hebrew Literature	6
Classical Biblical Philosophy	3
Classical Biblical Ethics	3
Public Speaking	3
Jewish History	6

The Association of Advanced Rabbinical and Talmudic Schools is a nationally recognized accrediting agency.

STUDY ABROAD

If you are eligible, study abroad programs may also allow you to apply for Federal and State financial aid, which can be applied to your tuition.

For more information on study abroad programs, please contact the appropriate school(s) directly:

Hebrew Theological College:
(847) 982-2500
YU/ S. Daniel Abraham Israel Program:
(212) 960-5277
Touro College Israel Option:
(718) 252-7800

Yeshivas and Seminaries in Eretz Yisroel do not generally have the status of an accredited college; i.e., they are not recognized by the Ministry of Education as degree granting institutions. While it may be that at the end of your yeshiva/seminary year, you will receive a transcript listing your yeshiva/seminary courses and grades, few colleges will grant credit based solely on that yeshiva/seminary transcript. However, all is not lost. There are several colleges that give students an opportunity to enroll in a study abroad program. This option is particularly helpful for students going to a yeshiva or seminary in Israel. These colleges have affiliations with yeshivas and seminaries in Israel and allow the student to earn credits which are transcripted on an American college transcript. To take advantage of this option you must apply for study abroad programs prior to beginning your studies in Israel.

You will need to contact the appropriate program to find out their deadlines, program requirements and application procedure. In addition to applying by the deadline, you may also need SAT scores and letters of recommendation.

Examples of colleges offering Israel study

options include, HTC/Teachers' Institute-Israel Experience Program, YU/ Stern S. Daniel Abraham Israel Program and Touro College-Israel Option (TCIO). These schools are all regionally accredited. Students who have been officially accepted into such programs will, at the end of their seminary year, receive an official transcript from the relevant college. Technically, such students are co-registered as both a yeshiva/seminary student and a student at the sponsoring college. Many colleges and universities will grant transfer credit for studies recorded on these college transcripts. You should note that after the yeshiva/seminary year, one does not necessarily have to attend the college that provides the transcript to receive transfer credit. However, you may wish to discuss this with the college at the time of application.

If you earned college credit from a non-US college, and it does not have US based accreditation or recognition, you may need to have your transcript evaluated by a foreign credential evaluator. Generally, a course-by-course assessment must be completed. However, be sure to call the college you plan to transfer to and make sure a foreign credential evaluation is required.

- Educational Credential Evaluators (ECE), www.ece.org, PO Box 514070, Milwaukee, WI 53203-3470, (414)-289-3400
- Josef Silny & Associates, www.jsilny.com, 7101 SW 102 Avenue, Miami, FL 33173, (305) 273-1616
- World Education Services (WES), www.wes.org, Bowling Green Station, P.O. Box 5087, New York, NY 10274-5087, (212) 966-6311

Charter Oak State College recognizes Educational Credential Evaluators (ECE) and World Education Services (WES). Excelsior College requires students to use Educational Credential Evaluators (ECE), while transcripts from Israeli institutions should be evaluated by Josef Silny & Associates.

NONCOLLEGIATE COURSES AND EXAMS

National PONSI and the American Council on Education (ACE) are agencies that assess courses at non-degree-granting institutions. If National PONSI or ACE decides that an institution's studies are at the college level, they will recommend that colleges accept these studies for college credit.

National PONSI, as a program of the Board of Regents of The University of the State of New York, the most comprehensive educational organization in the nation, has been highly successful in obtaining academic recognition for non-collegiate learning experiences for over 30 years. More than 1,500 colleges and universities currently report willingness to consider awarding credit based on National PONSI's credit recommendations. Member organizations include some of the best known names in corporate America, as well as labor unions, government agencies, professional and voluntary organizations, cultural institutions, and healthcare organizations.

The American Council on Education's College Credit Recommendation Service (CREDIT) connects workplace learning with colleges and universities by helping adults gain access to academic credit for formal courses and examinations taken outside traditional degree programs. For over 30 years, colleges and universities have trusted ACE to provide reliable course equivalency information to facilitate credit award decisions. Corporations, labor unions, professional and volunteer associations, schools, training suppliers, and government agencies, offering courses participate in the ACE CREDIT program.

Each of these agencies has evaluated courses or exams at many noncollegiate organizations and institutions. This includes industry coursework such as educational programs offered for employees at major corporations. They have also examined the courses at yeshivas and seminaries. National PONSI has reviewed, and recommended for credit, selected courses at Mercaz Hatorah, Toras Moshe, and Yeshiva Shaarei Torah. Ma'alot and Neve-affiliated seminaries also have had their coursework evaluated by ACE. The Cope Institute in New York, a division of Agudath Israel of America, offers a junior accounting program which has been recommended for 21 credits by ACE

In addition to yeshivas who have had their programs evaluated, there are other organizations that offer distance learning courses and proficiency exams that have been recommended for college credit and that can transfer to colleges. Teaching & Training International (TTI), based in New York, administers a number of exams that they refer to as JSE's Jewish Subject Exams. Another organization offering Judaic related courses is AHS Institute. AHS offers traditional courses, distance learning courses and challenge exams in a variety of subject areas. More information on TTI and AHS can be found in the "Community Programs" section later on in this book.

Some colleges also have their faculty approve exams and credentials for college credit. These include IT exams and credentials, including Oracle, Sun and Microsoft certification examinations, and EMT, aviation, and nursing certifications. Even if your courses or exams were not evaluated you may be able to have them evaluated through the prior learning assessment or portfolio process, which is discussed in the next section.

PRIOR LEARNING ASSESSMENT

Life experience credits:

"It's not how you know it but rather whether you know it."

Going back to our example of the teacher seeking credit: being a teacher doesn't mean you know how to teach. Of course most teachers know how to teach, but we all know at least one teacher who doesn't have a clue and has no business being in the classroom, especially at the front of the class.

See that? It didn't even come from me. Just sitting in shiur like a Golem doesn't help. You have to actually learn. I couldn't have said it better myself.

"Credit for life experience"—it's a misnomer. Here's the story.

"I have been a teacher for the last five years. Don't I deserve some credit? I know how to teach. I attended some lectures on pedagogy and methodology. I even received a teaching award." Slow down, the answer to your question is that you may deserve credit. However, you are approaching it all wrong.

Prior learning assessment or portfolio assessment is often very misunderstood by students. Let's take the teaching example above. Many colleges have a program to assess a student's prior learning. Notice what was just said, prior "**learning,**" emphasis on the learning. A legitimate portfolio or prior learning assessment program does not grant credit for your experiences. Rather, it grants credit for your college level knowledge.

Take a look at this statement from Excelsior College.

> *"If you have acquired degree-related, college-level learning through your work, community, volunteer, or other experiences, you may be a good candidate for portfolio-based assessment. Your advisor will recommend the portfolio assess-*

ment program that is best suited to your particular assessment goals and provide you with additional information about how to proceed. Please be aware that these assessments are not evaluations of life experience; rather, they are assessments of college-level learning gained as a result of that experience."

Notice that the emphasis is on the knowledge and not the experience.

Here's a statement from Charter Oak State College.

"Note that credit is awarded for the knowledge gained, not for the experience itself, which is no guarantee of learning. Attending a 4-week training program doesn't ensure that you will learn what is taught in the classes, so we can't award credit on the basis of your attendance certificate alone. Just as students who sit in a classroom are asked to provide evidence of their learning through term papers and tests, you are asked to provide proof that you really do have the knowledge you claim. Being able to show evidence that you were there and that college-level material was being presented is a step in the right direction. But such evidence must be bolstered by demonstration of the knowledge you've

You may have some wonderful talents, such as the ability to eat five bowls of chulent during Thursday night mishmar. As impressive as that may be, sadly it does not warrant college credit.

PRIOR LEARNING ASSESSMENT IS ALSO KNOWN AS CREDIT FOR LIFELONG LEARNING OR PORTFOLIO ASSESSMENT.

gained. The portfolio process is your opportunity to demonstrate that knowledge."

Once again, we see that the emphasis is on the actual learning or knowledge and not the experience.

We should also point out that you can only be awarded credit for college-level knowledge. Generally speaking, the areas in which you seek to earn credit must have a counterpart in some regionally accredited college.

As part of the portfolio process, some colleges require you, the student, to find a course title and description from a college catalog or website that matches the area in which you seek to earn credit.

Charter Oak State College and Excelsior College have a course to help guide you through the process. You earn credit for the course itself and have the opportunity to begin an actual portfolio as well. Following successful completion of the course, you are eligible to prepare and submit additional portfolios.

The portfolio process is not for the faint of heart, but it is a wonderful way to earn college credit in areas in which you have knowledge. If you have college level knowledge in Jewish subjects, whether from yeshiva, seminary, attending *shiurim*, or personal study you can use the portfolio process to earn credit for your knowledge.

IN CONCLUSION, WE DON'T MEAN TO BASH "EXPERIENCE." EXPERIENCE IS IMPORTANT, AND IS OFTEN PART OF THE PORTFOLIO PROCESS. FIRST, YOUR EXPERIENCES WILL HELP GIVE YOU A STARTING POINT IN TERMS OF EXAMINING YOUR KNOWLEDGE. SECONDLY, IT CAN BE USED TO HELP SET THE CONTEXT OF AND DOCUMENT YOUR KNOWLEDGE.

WHO NEEDS A DEGREE?

When prospective students call to discuss their degree options, they often ask why, in fact, they need a degree. *"After all,"* they say, *"look at all those people who are successful in business and other fields yet never earned a degree."* There doesn't seem to be a simple answer to their question. It is true that a great many people were successful in supporting their families and even built business empires without having set foot in college. On the other hand, the data comparing the income of people with varying levels of education show that individuals who earned a bachelor's degree earn more, on average, than those with limited or no higher education.

My response to students asking this question is that they have a good point, and that in fact the college degree is not necessarily the key to, or a failsafe indicator of, future success. However, I explain that if you look at the help wanted section of a major newspaper, you may be surprised by the type and number of jobs and positions that require a bachelor's degree just to apply for the job. This is the case even for the most mundane jobs and positions. *"Why?"* prospective students ask. I respond that many employers utilize the bachelor's degree as part of the screening process. A degree should indicate that the applicant possess at least a minimum educational level and skill set that could be applied to the workplace, regardless of the position or job. I was pleased to learn that I was not alone in this thought process. Charles Murray, the W.H. Brady Scholar at the American Enterprise Institute in Washington, D.C. and best-selling coauthor of The Bell Curve, writes in his new book Real Education, *"Economists have established beyond doubt that people with BA degrees (using the term BA to represent all four-year traditional undergraduate degrees) earn more on average than peo-ple without them."* *"But why"* he asks, *"does the BA produce that result?"* Murray goes on to explain, *"Employers value the BA because it is a no cost (for them) screening device for academic ability and perseverance... Knowing this, large numbers of students are in college to buy their admission ticket—the BA."*

Now, please don't misunderstand my point. I am not in any manner devaluing the worth of a college education. I'm just wondering aloud as to its importance and its appropriateness, as a norm, for the majority of prospective students. Too many people choose to pursue a BA simply for its artificial economic– screening– value rather than its educational or intrinsic economic value. This would be fine if there is a link between the education and the economics. However, as stated above, many employers simply use the BA as a screening device, not necessarily valuing the educational implications of the degree. As Murray states in his book, *"Employers do not value what the student learned, just that the student has a degree."*

As you read through this book you will see the terms "liberal arts" or "arts and sciences" sprinkled throughout. In many cases at least 50%, and even closer to 75%, of your degree will consist of liberal arts courses. This is true even when your focus of study may be in a professional field such as business or accounting. Therefore, a liberal arts education will be a major part of your degree whether you like it or not. Basically, the student is often compelled to acquire the undergraduate degree, simply for its screening value, even when it may make no apparent educational or intrinsic economic sense.

Here is how Murray ends his chapter titled *"Too Many People are Going to College."*

"Imagine that America had no system of postsecondary education and you were made a member of a task force assigned to create one from scratch. Ask yourself what you would think if one of your colleagues submitted this proposal:

First, we will set up a common goal for every young person that represents educational success. We will call it the BA. We will then make it difficult or impossible for most people to achieve this goal. For those who can, achieving the goal will take four years no matter what is being taught. We will attach an economic reward for reaching the goal that often has little to do with the content of what is being learned. We will lure large numbers of people who do not possess adequate ability or motivation to try and achieve the goal and then fail. We will then stigmatize everyone who fails to achieve it.

What I have just described is the system we have in place. There must be a better way."

On the other hand, a wise man pointed out that a general education will help people better relate to others and deal more effectively in their jobs. A broader education may better equip you to deal with others by establishing some common ground in the workplace. If, for example, your client or supervisor has an interest in history, some knowledge of history on your part gives you an opening to make conversation, which may lead to a better business relationship. Recently, an attorney told me that he would no longer hire any law associates unless they had earned a secular under-graduate degree. He explained that even if they graduate from good law schools, he is often frustrated by their lack of communication skills and computer savvy. The knowledge of the law is important, but so is the ability to effectively communicate thoughts in a letter or memo, as well as being able to use basic computer software within the practice of law.

The bottom line is that we all agree education is important. After all, we learn in the Mishnah in tractate Avos, *"Who is wise? He who learns from everyone."* Education and knowledge is valuable. We can learn from everyone. How that education is related to our ability to perform our career or job skills is open to debate, as is the intrinsic economic value of that education. However, this book was not written in an attempt to change our educational system, only to show how to better use the system to reach your goal.

Nontraditional degree programs help to alleviate some of the concerns discussed above and described by Murray. Even Murray writes that he is primarily taking issue with the four-year traditional residential college education. Nontraditional colleges and degree programs, along with credit-by-exam programs, recognize that not all students are created equal; students have varying academic abilities, goals and desires. Nontraditional educational options give students the flexibility to take some control of their education, focusing on areas they feel are most important to their own goals, while earning the coveted BA. Even that attorney, mentioned above, would feel comfortable hiring a law associate with a nontraditional—distance learning—undergraduate degree.

So now you can understand why you need that BA—whether or not it may make any intrinsic economic or educational sense. In fact, it may have more intrinsic value than you had previously thought. In any case, remember, you can always change our postsecondary educational system after you earn your DEGREE.

Section 7

THE COLLEGES

❦

Charter Oak State College

Excelsior College

THE COLLEGES

In this next section you are introduced to the colleges: Charter Oak State College and Excelsior College. We begin with a general overview for each college. We then move on and examine the components of each colleges' degree program. The information for this section was drawn from both college's websites and catalogs. The opinions, interpretation, and application of the information are based on the understanding of this author and should not be construed as the official policy of the college.

Both of these colleges allow students the maximum flexibility in terms of designing their own degree and earning credit. All the credits needed to earn the degree may be transferred in from other sources. This means there is no residency requirement and technically you do not have to take any of the many online, CD, or video courses offered by each institution. However, as we have described at the beginning of this book, this does not mean there are no rules. You must follow each college's distribution requirement and only credits from approved sources will be accepted in transfer.

Application

The general application procedure and fee structure is similar for each of these colleges. The application process is simple and straightforward. You complete an application along with the application fee and have official copies of your transcripts sent directly from each credit source. I must stress that these transcripts should be sent directly to the college from each originating institution or organization. Approximately 4-6 weeks after receipt of your application and transcripts, you should receive notification of your acceptance and a preliminary unofficial review of all your transfer credits. The college will let you know which credits are accepted and how these credits basically fit into the degree plan selected.

Fees

There are 3 general fees associated with each of these colleges and that are applicable to all students: application fee, enrollment or matriculation fee and the eagerly awaited graduation fee. The enrollment or matriculation fee covers the official evaluation of transfer credits and a year of student advising.

When to Enroll

Many students delay enrolling in the college of their choice until they feel that they are within a year of graduation. This is done to minimize the cost of enrollment as there is a yearly enrollment fee. However, this fee is about half of the initial year's enrollment fee. I generally suggest students consider enrolling if they are within two years of graduation, assuming it is a financially feasible alternative. My thinking is as follows: while you, the student, can begin planning your degree without enrolling, there are questions that come up as you take courses and exams. Additionally, the college policies can and do occasionally change, and students are grandfathered into the policies in effect at the time of enrollment. These changes can at times set you back several months as you scramble to rearrange your degree plan to fit any new policies that may have been placed into effect. I therefore view the cost for the extra year of enrollment as an insurance policy. You decide.

As of July 2008 the fees are as follows:

Fees	Charter Oak*	Excelsior
Application	$75	$75
Enrollment	$1335	$895
Graduation	$205	$495
Enrollment add. yr.	$685	$440

* fees listed are for non-Connecticut residents

Other Fees

The fees discussed above are limited to administrative and academic advisement. The other major costs of the degree are the actual courses or exams. These costs can vary widely depending on where the courses are actually taken. Both Charter Oak and Excelsior offer a comprehensive number of courses online and should be considered by students. The costs for the various exams have already been discussed earlier in this book in the section on testing. In terms of cost, the bottom line is that the degree programs discussed in this book are relatively light on the wallet or pocketbook.

CHARTER OAK STATE COLLEGE

Students matriculating in Charter Oak after July 2009 will be required to complete a three-credit capstone experience. More information can be found in Appendix C.

ABOUT CHARTER OAK STATE COLLEGE

Charter Oak State College was established in 1973 by the Connecticut Legislature to provide an alternative way for adults to earn associate's and bachelor's (baccalaureate) degrees. The College is accredited by the Connecticut Board of Governors for Higher Education and the New England Association of Schools and Colleges.

Charter Oak is a distance learning college offering both video and online courses. A major Charter Oak advantage is the many ways that credits can be combined to form a degree. Students can also earn credits through:

- Courses transferred from other regionally accredited colleges and universities
- Standardized tests (CLEP, DANTES)
- Corporate & agency training programs evaluated by the ACE / PONSI
- Military service schools and occupational ratings evaluated by ACE
- Faculty-evaluated licensures / certifications
- Contract learning (independent study)
- Portfolio assessment (experiential learning)
- Connecticut Credit Assessment Program (CCAP)

Students who matriculate (enroll as a degree candidate) at Charter Oak State College work with an Academic Counselor to create a personalized degree that takes into account their prior college experience, preferred method of earning credits, and future academic goals.

Degree requirements are satisfied in a variety of different ways. As a result, there is no specific list of courses that every student must take. While this is different from what you would experience at a traditional college, it provides adult learners with additional flexibility as they work with their Academic Counselor to plan their degree program. All degree planning can be accomplished via e-mail, mail, phone and/or fax.

After reviewing the information on the college website, www.charteroak.edu, prospective students with questions should contact the Admissions Office. Matriculated (enrolled) students should consult the additional resources available on the Academics page.

Student Body

Approximately 2,000 students are enrolled (matriculated) with the College, representing all 50 states and 9 countries.

Programs of Study

The College offers four General Studies Degrees—Associate in Arts and Associate in Science degrees (requiring a minimum of 60 credits), and Bachelor of Arts and Bachelor of Science degrees (requiring at least 120 credits). Every degree awarded at Charter Oak is customized based on the student's educational background and goals. There are also professional Certificate Programs (in Project Management, Computer Security, and Public Safety Administration), and more than 150 video and online courses.

Graduates

Even though over 90% of the students are employed, close to 50% of recent Charter Oak graduates have gone on to graduate school. In addition, 45% of graduates report professional advancement as a result of their Charter Oak degree.

The information in this section is quoted and adapted from
Charter Oak State College's website and publications.

A degree from Charter Oak requires more than the simple accumulation of 60 credits for the associate degree and 120 credits for the baccalaureate degree. All students must complete Distributive Requirements, which include General Education requirements as well as a minimum number of credits in Liberal Arts. Baccalaureate degree candidates must also complete a faculty-approved Concentration of 36 credits or more.

In a nutshell, the Charter Oak degree is made up of several parts:

- *Associate in Arts/Science*
- *General Education Requirement*
- *Electives*
- *Bachelor of Arts/Science*
- *General Education Requirement*
- *Concentration Requirement*
- *Electives*

ASSOCIATE DEGREE OVERVIEW

You may earn an Associate in Arts or Associate in Science degree. Both degrees are in General Studies and require 60 semester credits, including the completion of general education requirements. The Associate in Arts degree requires 45 liberal arts credits, while the Associate in Science degree requires 30. There is usually plenty of room for open electives.

BACHELOR'S (BACCALAUREATE) DEGREE OVERVIEW

You may earn a Bachelor of Arts or Bachelor of Science degree. Both baccalaureate degrees are in General Studies and require 120 semester credits. In addition to satisfying general education requirements, the Bachelor of Arts degree requires 90 liberal arts credits, while the Bachelor of Science degree requires 60. Bachelor's Degree seeking students must also complete a "Concentration" in a specific discipline or combination of disciplines.

CONCENTRATION BASICS

A concentration consists of a minimum of 36 credits in one or more fields of study. Concentrations can be in specific subject areas like Business Administration, Child Studies, Psychology or Health Care Administration; or they can be multidisciplinary if you have a background or interest in related subject areas. The multidisciplinary concentrations, called Individualized Studies and Liberal Studies, are popular with students who have very specific or unique career interests because they can be customized based on those interests.

Additionally, at least 50% of the credits must be in the Liberal Arts and Sciences for an Associates in Science or Bachelors of Science and at least 75% of the credits must be in the Liberal Arts and Sciences for an Associates in Arts or Bachelors of Arts.

GENERAL EDUCATION

Here we will take a look at the General Education requirements for Charter Oak State College. To satisfy the general education requirement, you have to satisfy the requirements listed for each category. Remember, this is a listing of categories and not of courses. Many different courses may satisfy any given category. In the listing below, examples of some of the courses that can satisfy each category are given. Many times, exams can also satisfy a category. A list of which exams fulfill each category can be found later on in this guide. Additionally, some courses can satisfy the requirements of two or more categories.

This General Education requirement is intended to ensure that students gain the knowledge to further develop their potential and enhance their capability to engage in a lifelong process of learning. By fulfilling this requirement, students acquire knowledge of American history and the culture of another country; an understanding of a global society and their relation to it; an understanding of how the social and behavioral sciences inform us of past and future efforts; a sense of social, ethical and cultural values; and an appreciation of how the arts and humanities enhance one's life. They also develop communication skills, critical thinking, information literacy, ethical decision-making, quantitative skills and an understanding of the scientific method.

If credits apply to more than one category, credits will be counted only once towards the total needed for the degree.

Skill Areas

Communication

Students will communicate effectively using Standard English, read and listen critically, and write and speak thoughtfully, clearly, coherently and persuasively.

Written Communication......................................6 cr

Examples: English Composition I and II, English Composition plus Technical Writing course or two writing-intensive courses, CLEP exam with essay, AP English/Language and Composition.

Oral Communication...3 cr

Example: Principles of Speech, Principles of Public Speaking.

Although the following three outcomes have a set number of credits attached to them, they can be met by taking specific courses or by demonstrating that these outcomes were part of other courses. These skills may be attained in liberal arts courses or concentration courses.

Critical Thinking...0-3 cr

Students will be able to organize, interpret, and evaluate ideas. May be met by taking any course in which a research paper, term paper, project or lab is required.

Information Literacy.....................................1-3 cr

Students will be able to locate, evaluate, synthesize and use information from a variety of sources and understand the ethical issues involved in accessing and using information. May be met by taking a course that requires the use of current technology for developing research or term papers, by taking a course in information literacy, or by taking on-line courses that require accessing information on line.

Ethical Decision-Making..3 cr

Student will be able to use critical thinking skills to make ethical decisions. May be met by taking a course that has a significant ethics component, by taking a series of courses that have an ethical component,
or by taking courses such as *Ethics, Business Ethics, Health Care Ethics,
or Computer Ethics.*

Knowledge Areas

U.S. History/Government..3 cr

Students will have an understanding of the ideas and processes that
shaped the history of the United States.

*Examples: American Government, American History, History of the
United States, The Civil War.*

Non-U.S. History or Culture..3 cr

Students will have an understanding of major developmentsin the
history and culture of other countries.

*Examples: any art, literature, history, foreign language or religion course,
Western Civilization I or II.*

Global Understanding..3 cr

Students will have an understanding of the impact of nations, regions
and cultures upon other nations, regions and cultures since 1945, and
the impact of these interactions upon individuals.

*Examples: Religions of the World, Cultural Anthropology, Comparative
Economic Systems, Comparative Political Systems, International Business, International Economics, International Marketing, Introduction
to Modern Middle East.*

Literature and Fine Arts............................3 cr

Students will demonstrate an understanding of the arts and literature, and gain an appreciation of their impact on our heritage and culture.

Examples: Music Appreciation, Art Appreciation, Art History, Music History, Theatre, Dance, Creative Writing, Drawing, Literature.

Social/Behavioral Sciences.......................3 cr

Students will gain an understanding of self and the world, of social and cultural institutions, and the interdependent influences of the individual, family, and society in shaping behavior.

Examples: Anthropology, criminal justice, communications, economics, gerontology, psychology, sociology, political science, communications (not Basic Speech).

Mathematics...3 cr

Students will have an understanding of mathematics beyond the entry-level requirements for college.

Examples: College-level algebra or higher.

Natural Science......................................4-6 cr

Students will understand the basic scientific process and theories and be able to apply scientific inquiry. One 4-credit course that includes a lab, or two 3-credit courses.

Examples: astronomy, biology, chemistry, environmental science, geology, oceanography, physical geography, physics.

A concentration is similar to a major, but it offers far more flexibility by allowing you to work with the credits you have already earned to map-out a degree program that meets your career and personal goals. The College's academic counselors and faculty will provide guidance in helping you choose credits to fulfill your concentration plan of study (CPS), but ultimately, you will need to explain the focus of your concentration and the manner in which credits you have selected fit into your concentration. In thinking about which concentration will work best for you, consider; your career goals, personal interests, when you want to complete your degree, and which credits you have already completed.

THE CONCENTRATION

For a bachelor's degree, students must complete a concentration. The college catalog, student handbook and website contain a listing of concentration options. There are three concentrations that may be of particular interest to the readers of this guide: Individualized Studies, Liberal Studies and Judaic Studies.

Baccalaureate Concentration

Through the Concentration Plan of Study process, each candidate for the bachelor's degree must establish and complete a faculty-approved concentration of 36 credits or more in a single subject area or combination of subject areas with which they demonstrate in-depth knowledge within one or more fields of study. At least 15 credits in the concentration (18 in Individualized Studies and Liberal Studies concentrations) must be at the upper (Junior/Senior) level. The remaining credits may be spread across the lower level (typically freshman and sophomore or 100/200) level. Acceptance of the concentration plan is dependent upon the faculty's approval of the proposed courses and the rationale presented by the student. Upon matriculation, a student will receive a copy of the *Student Handbook* from his/her academic counselor, who will assist with the planning process. The *Student Handbook* details ways in which specific concentration objectives can be met.

Individualized Studies

This concentration option allows students to combine professional studies with the liberal arts and sciences or a second professional studies area into a cohesive course of study. **The Individualized Studies concentration is not meant to serve merely as a convenient repository for a collection of assorted credits.** It provides the opportunity to integrate a broad range of accumulated knowledge and new learning into an interdisciplinary program which will meet an individual's career and/or personal needs.

The key to receiving approval for this concentration is the student's ability to explain the rationale for the proposed concentration and its relation to his or her career and/or personal goals.

The number of credits and distribution by level should consist of a minimum of 36 credits with a minimum of 18 at the upper level. The 18 upper level credits should represent a logical distribution from various disciplines in the concentration. The concentration needs to show breadth and depth in each subject area chosen.

Some sample concentrations:

Liberal Studies

This concentration is composed of traditional liberal arts disciplines found in the humanities, the social sciences, and the natural sciences and mathematics. Like the Individualized Studies concentration, the Liberal Studies concentration provides the opportunity to integrate a broad range of accumulated knowledge and new learning into an interdisciplinary program which will meet the student's career and/or personal needs.

The Liberal Studies concentration is not meant to serve merely as a convenient repository for a collection of assorted credits. The credits proposed should form a cohesive, coherent program of study. The number of credits and distribution by level are the same as those for the Individualized Studies concentration: a minimum of 36 credits with a minimum of 18 at the upper level. The 18 upper level credits should represent a logical distribution from the various disciplines in the concentration.

The key to receiving approval for this concentration is the same as that for the individualized studies concentration: the student's ability to explain the rationale underpinning the proposed concentration and its relation to his or her career and/or personal goals.

Judaic Studies

The Judaic Studies concentration will include such areas as the Bible, Talmud, Law, Ethics, Religious Thought, Philosophy, Literature, Hebrew, and History. Students will be exposed to a variety of texts both ancient/classical and contemporary. Students will have the opportunity to study these subjects and gain a knowledge and understanding of the textual materials as well as critical thinking and analytical skills that can be used in other disciplines. Students must also demonstrate proficiency in reading and translating Hebrew through Hebrew language courses or courses that use Hebrew texts.

Concentration Requirements:

Bible ....3 cr

Law ....3 cr

Philosophy/Ethics ....3 cr

History ....3 cr

Talmud ....3 cr

Judaism and Contemporary Society ....3 cr

Examples: Judaism and Business or Judaism and Medical Ethics

Literature ....3 cr

Electives** ....15 cr

Prerequisites:

Hebrew ....6 cr

*** Must relate to concentration*

Student Learning Outcomes:

Students who graduate with a concentration in Judaic Studies should be able to:

1) read and utilize primary and secondary source materials;

2) critically interpret Judaic concepts;

3) discuss the historical development of Judaism as a world religion (e.g., Ancient Judaism, Medieval Judaism, the Haskala [Jewish Enlightenment] and the encounter with modernity);

4) demonstrate an appreciation and understanding of the significance of the Torah, Talmud and Bible in Judaism and their place in contemporary society;

5) use critical and analytical thinking skills in applying theory to practice; and

6) demonstrate a foundation in Jewish law and tradition, and the skills to approach the texts independently.

STATUS REPORTS

In this section we will take a look at some Status Reports. There are two types of reports: unofficial reports given as part of the application and acceptance process, and official reports generated upon enrollment or matriculation to the college. The official status reports are updated periodically as you transfer in your coursework or exams.

The status reports in this section are not necessarily the full report for a given student. Only sections were copied, but they are taken from actual reports issued to students. The idea of this section is to give you real world view and help you visualize how courses and exams fit into the degree program.

These reports are reproduced for illustrative purposes only.

Charter Oak State College Status Report Sample

Charter Oak
STATE COLLEGE

Degrees Without Boundaries

Charter Oak State College
55 Paul J. Manafort Drive
New Britain, CT 06053-2150
860-832-3800 Fax 860-832-3999

STATUS REPORT

Bachelor of Science

Page 1 of 3

Student ID :

Area of Concentration: Individualized Studies

The student attended a seminary in Israel as part of a study abroad program with a US regionally accredited college. This allowed the student to transfer her credits as discussed earlier in the Study Abroad section.

Course Number and Description		Level Code	Grade	Test Score Pct	General Education	Lib. Arts	Non-Lib. Arts	Qual.	DUP
Hebrew Theological College - Skokie, IL									
Beginning 2005-2006									
Transfer									
BIBL 111	The Pentateuch With Commentaries 1		A			3	0	12.00	
BIBL 112	The Pentateuch With Commentaries 2		A			3	0	12.00	
BIBL 141	Introduction To Early Prophets 1		A		X	3	0	12.00	
BIBL 142	Introduction To Early Prophets 2		A-		X	3	0	11.10	
BIBL 201	Advanced Torah: Genesis 1		A			3	0	12.00	
BIBL 202	Advanced Torah: Genesis 2		A			3	0	12.00	
BIBL 226	Readings In Prophets & Hagiographa		A			2	0	8.00	
BIBL 255	Later Prophets: Ezekiel 1		A			2	0	8.00	
HIST 203	Topics In Contemp Jewish History		A-		X	2	0	7.40	
JLAW 127	Introduction To Shabbat Laws		A			2	0	8.00	
JLAW 227	Sabbath Laws		A			2	0	8.00	
PHIL 208	The Philosophy Of Prayer 1		A			2	0	8.00	

She took an online Charter Oak Chemistry course. Note that Charter Oak offers some online courses with a lab component that can be completed at home.

Charter Oak State College - New Britain, CT
2006-2007

Spring

CHE 101 02	I Introduction To Chemistry With Lab		B+		y	X	4	0	13.20

She also took several Judaic AHS courses or exams.

Association for Hebraic Studies * - Suffern, NY
Beginning 2007-2008

Transfer

JLW 424	Sabbath 5	U	A		3	0	12.00
JLW 430	Dietary Law 1	U	A		3	0	12.00
JLW 431	Dietary Law 2	U	A		3	0	12.00

She took some CLEPs and a DANTES/DSST exam. Note the letter designations in the General Education column. This indicates which of the requirements were satisfied with each exam.

College Level Examination Program *
Beginning 2007-2008

Transfer

CS03B	History Of United States 2 (50)6/07	P		u	X	3	0	0
CS05	Analyzing & Interpreting Lit (63) 3/07	P		a	X	6	0	0

DANTES Examinations *
Beginning 2007-2008

Transfer

SE826	Principles Of Public Speaking (5/07)	P		o	X	3	0	0

Here are two online self-paced courses that she took through UC Berkeley Extension.

University of California-Berkeley - Berkeley, CA
Beginning 2007-2008

Fall

CHEM X18	Introductory Organic Chemistry		B		X	3	0	9.00

Spring

MCELLBI X105	Introductory Biochemistry	U	A-		X	3	0	11.10

The report concludes with a summary section. Here the required distribution of credits is tallied and the General Education requirements are listed and noted if they were satisfied or not. Also note that the number of Liberal Arts and non-Liberal Arts credits are calculated.

Requirements: Bachelor of Science	Required	Earned
Minimum Semester Credits	120	117.0
Minimum Liberal Arts	60	117.0
Credits Beyond Two Years	30	110.0

Concentration Completed: Y

Academic Autobiography Submitted: Y
Academic Autobiography Approved: Y

0

	Total	COSC
Total Credts with Grades:	75.00	7.0
Total Quality Points:	281.80	22.20
Quality Point Average:	3.757	3.17

General Education Requirement	Outcome Met
(a) Literature/Fine Arts	Y
(b) Behavioral Science	Y
(d) Ethical Decision Making	Y
(e) Written Communication	Y
(g) Global Understanding	N
(y) Information Literacy	Y
(q) Mathematics	Y
(n) Non-U.S. History and Culture	Y
(o) Oral Communication	Y
(s) Natural Science	Y
(u) U.S. History and Government	Y
(X) General Education credits	

Liberal Arts: 117.00
Non-Liberal Arts: .00
Total Credits Earned: 117.00

Advisor: ▉
Email: ▉
Phone: ▉

Matriculation Status: Matriculation Renewal
Begin Date: ▉
Expiration Date: ▉

Sample 2

This student took some CLEPs and Excelsior College exams. Note the letter designations in the General Education column, this indicates which of the requirements were satisfied with each exam.

Excelsior College   - Albany, NY
Beginning 2006-2007

    Transfer

INL 102	Information Literacy	P		y	X	0	1	(

College Level Examination Program *
Beginning 2006-2007

    Transfer

CG03	College Mathematics (63) 07/06	P		q	X	6	0	(
CS08	Biology (71) 12/06	P			X	6	0	(
CS24	Chemistry (50) 09/06	P		s	X	6	0	(
CS25	Introductory Psychology (71) 08/06	P			X	3	0	(
CS38	Introductory Sociology (71) 10/06	P		b	X	3	0	(

Excelsior College Examinations *
Beginning 2006-2007

    Transfer

434	English Composition	A		e	X	6	0	24.0(

Sample 3

The student took advantage of the college courses offered by his mesivta. Courses were offered through Mercy and STAQ.

Course Number and Description		Level Code	Grade	Test Score Pct	General Education	Lib. Arts	Non-Lib. Arts	Qual.	DUP
Mercy College - **Dobbs Ferry, NY**									
Beginning 1998-1999									
Transfer									
ECON 220	Macroeconomics	B	B		I	3	0	9.00	
ENGL 315	Shakespeare		B		A	3	0	9.00	
GOVT 101	Political Power In America		B		W	3	0	9.00	
HUMN 220	Comedy, Wit & Humor		B			3	0	9.00	
PHSC 110	Introduction To Geology		B		S	4	0	12.00	
St. Thomas Aquinas College - **Sparkill, NY**									

He learned in Eretz Yisroel where his yeshiva had their courses evaluated by National PONSI allowing him to transfer almost sixty credits. Below are just some of the courses transferred to Charter Oak.

Course Number and Description		Level Code	Grade	Test Score Pct	General Education	Lib. Arts	Non-Lib. Arts	Qual.	DUP
Mercaz Hatorah * - **Jerusalem, Israel**									
Beginning 1999-2000									
Transfer									
B 101	Studies In The Pentateuch	I	A			3	0	12.00	
B 201	Adv St: Pentateuch & Midrashic Lit	U	B			3	0	9.00	
P: RE 101	St: Trad Jewish Thought/ethics	I	A		C	3	0	12.00	
P: RE 201	Duties Of The Heart:trust In G-d	I	B			3	0	9.00	
T 015	Survey Bava Kama	U	A			4	0	16.00	
T 016	Survey Bava Metzia	U	A			4	0	16.00	
T 019	Survey Kidushin 2	U	A			1	0	4.00	
T 024	Survey Pesachim	U	A			2	0	8.00	
T 026	Survey Makot	U	A			1	0	4.00	
T 028	Survey Sanhedrin	U	A			2	0	8.00	
T 136	Kidushin 2-first Year	I	B			2	0	6.00	

He also took several AHS distance learning courses while learning in yeshiva in the US, as well as an online course from Charter Oak.

Course Number and Description		Level Code	Grade	Test Score Pct	General Education	Lib. Arts	Non-Lib. Arts	Qual.	DUP
Association for Hebraic Studies * - **Suffern, NY**									
Beginning 2007-2008									
Transfer									
JLW 424	Sabbath 5	U	A			3	0	12.00	
JLW 430	Dietary Law 1	U	A			3	0	12.00	
JLW 431	Dietary Law 2	U	A			3	0	12.00	

EXCELSIOR COLLEGE

ABOUT EXCELSIOR COLLEGE

Excelsior College helps busy working adults earn the degrees they need with flexible distance education programs.

The College, formerly Regents College, was founded in 1971 on the fundamental philosophy that what you know is more important than where or how you learned it. The College recognizes that adult learners can attain college-level knowledge in many ways. Excelsior, which means "Ever Upward," depicts how, with over 125,000 graduates, the College propels students just like you toward their goals.

A World Leader in Distance Education

As a world leader in distance education, the college credit you have already earned, is applied to a respected degree in Liberal Arts, Business, Technology, Nursing, or Health Sciences—giving you the best start toward degree completion.

As an Excelsior College student, you will advance with a customized degree completion plan and choose from among many credit-earning options:

- Distance courses from Excelsior College and other regionally accredited institutions
- Traditional courses at a campus near you
- For-credit exams including Excelsior College Examinations
- Portfolio Assessment, which can allow credit earned from work, community or volunteer experiences
- Programs reviewed by the New York State Board of Regents National Program on Non-collegiate Sponsored Instruction (National PONSI)
- In accordance with Excelsior College policies and procedures, students may appeal for consideration of degree-level credit from non-regionally accredited schools by Excelsior College faculty.
- Association of Advanced Rabbinical and Talmudic Schools (limited)

♦ Graduates advance ever upward to graduate schools and better jobs in business, government, and health care. Find out how close you already are to the degree you need and how far you can go with Excelsior College.

How It Works

From start to finish, Excelsior College gives you an efficient and affordable way to earn the college degree you need while meeting your family and work commitments.

Start by applying. Your application will enable the College to prepare an unofficial evaluation of your prior learning that indicates which of your prior credits are likely to transfer. You will then receive an enrollment packet that will enable you to matriculate into the College. Excelsior College staff can assist with any questions you may have during this process.

When you enroll, a team of experienced Academic Advisors works with you to develop a degree completion plan, so you can finish with the mix of courses and exams (including dozens of Excelsior College courses and Excelsior College Exams) that fit your program, learning style, budget, and schedule.

The information in this section is quoted and adapted from Excelsior College's website and publications.

THE ASSOCIATE IN ARTS DEGREE

The Associate in Arts degree requires at least 60 credits. However, this does not mean you can just put together a hodgepodge of any 60 credits and expect to be granted a degree. The 60 credits must meet the distribution requirements for the degree program which you select. Here are some of those requirements:

Written English	**3 credits**
General Education	**33 credits**

The general education requirement is made up of three distribution areas:

Humanities, Social Sciences/History and Natural Sciences/Mathematics.

You must earn 12 credits in two distribution areas and 9 in the remaining area.

Information Literacy	**1 credit**
Electives	**23 credits**
Arts & Sciences	12 credits
Arts & Sciences or Applied professional	11 credits

For the Associates in Arts degree at least 48 of the 60 credits must be in the arts and sciences area.

AA Degree Requirements

Written English 3 credits
Information Literacy 1 credit

General Education

You must have a minimum of 33 credits distributed among Humanities, Social Sciences/History and Natural Sciences/Mathematics; 12 credits in two areas and 9 in the other.

Humanities	12
Social Sciences/History	12
Natural Sciences/Mathematics	9

Or

Humanities	9
Social Sciences/History	12
Natural Sciences/Mathematics	12

Or

Humanities	12
Social Sciences/History	9
Natural Sciences/Mathematics	12

THE ASSOCIATE IN SCIENCE DEGREE

The Associate in Science degree requires at least 60 credits. However, this does not mean you can just put together a hodgepodge of any 60 credits and expect to be granted a degree. The 60 credits must meet the distribution requirements for the degree program which you select. Here are some of those requirements:

Written English	3 credits
General Education	24 credits

The general education requirement is made up of three distribution areas:

Humanities, Social Sciences/History and Natural Sciences/Mathematics.

You must earn 9 credits in two distribution areas and 6 in the remaining area.

Information Literacy	1 credit
Electives	32 credits
Arts & Sciences	3 credits
Arts & Sciences or Applied professional	29 credits

For the Associates in Arts degree at least 30 of the 60 credits must be in the arts and sciences area.

AS Degree Requirements

Written English	3 credits
Information Literacy	1 credit

General Education

You must have a minimum of 24 credits distributed among Humanities, Social Sciences/History and Natural Sciences/Mathematics; 9 credits in two areas and 6 in the other.

Humanities	9
Social Sciences/History	9
Natural Sciences/Mathematics	6

Or

Humanities	6
Social Sciences/History	9
Natural Sciences/Mathematics	9

Or

Humanities	9
Social Sciences/History	6
Natural Sciences/Mathematics	9

THE BACHELOR'S OF ARTS DEGREE

BA Degree Requirements

Written English	3 credits
Information Literacy	1 credit

General Education
You must have a minimum of 33 credits distributed among Humanities, Social Sciences/History and Natural Sciences/Mathematics; 12 credits in two areas and 9 in the other.

Humanities	12
Social Sciences/History	12
Natural Sciences/ Mathematics	9

Or

Humanities	9
Social Sciences/History	12
Natural Sciences/ Mathematics	12

Or

Humanities	12
Social Sciences/History	9
Natural Sciences/ Mathematics	12

Liberal Studies Option
You must demonstrate expertise by certifying depth of knowledge in at least two different Arts and Sciences disciplines or subject areas. Each depth is made up of at least 12 credits with at least 3 at the upper level.

Depth 1 (at least 3 upper level)	12
Depth 2 (at least 3 upper level)	12

Electives
After you satisfy the specific degree requirements as listed above you can round out your degree with elective credits.

Arts and Sciences and Upper Level Requirements
60 of the total credits must be in the arts and sciences, at least 21 must be at the upper level.

For the Bachelor's in Arts degree, we start with the same requirements found for the Associates in Arts:

Written English	**3 credits**
Information Literacy	**1 credits**
General Education	**33 credits**

The general education requirement is made up of three distribution areas:

Humanities, Social Sciences/History and Natural Sciences/Mathematics. *

You must earn 12 credits in two distribution areas and 9 in the remaining area.

And add some more:

Depth Requirement

This requirement consists of two depth areas of at least 12 credits each. At least 3 of the 12 credits in each depth must be at the upper level.

For the Bachelors of Arts, the two depth areas must be in two different arts and sciences disciplines.

Additionally, for a Bachelor of Arts at least 90 credits must be in the arts and sciences with at least 30 of those at the upper level.

> *at least 2 credits of the Natural Sciences/Mathematics area must be in mathematics or statistics.

THE BACHELOR'S OF SCIENCE DEGREE

For the Bachelor's in Science degree, we start with the same requirements found for the Associates in Science:

Written English	**3 credits**
Information Literacy	**1 credits**
General Education	**24 credits**

The general education requirement is made up of three distribution areas:

Humanities, Social Sciences/History and Natural Sciences/Mathematics. *

You must earn 9 credits in two distribution areas and 6 in the remaining area.

And add some more:

Depth Requirement

This requirement consists of two depth areas of at least 12 credits each. At least 3 of the 12 credits in each depth must be at the upper level.

For a Bachelor in Science, one depth must be in the arts and sciences area. The second depth may be in another arts and sciences area or an applied professional area.

Additionally, for a Bachelor of Science 60 credits must be in the arts and sciences, with at least 21 of those at the upper level. An additional 9 upper level credits are required but can come from the arts and sciences or applied professional areas.

BS Degree Requirements

Written English	**3 credits**
Information Literacy	**1 credit**

General Education

You must have a minimum of 24 credits distributed among Humanities, Social Sciences/History and Natural Sciences/Mathematics; 9 credits in two areas and 6 in the other.

Humanities	**9**
Social Sciences/History	**9**
Natural Sciences/ Mathematics	**6**

Or

Humanities	**6**
Social Sciences/History	**9**
Natural Sciences/ Mathematics	**9**

Or

Humanities	**9**
Social Sciences/History	**6**
Natural Sciences/ Mathematics	**9**

Liberal Studies Option

You must demonstrate expertise by certifying depth of knowledge in at least two different disciplines or subject areas. Each depth is made up of at least 12 credits with at least 3 at the upper level.

Depth 1 (at least 3 upper level)	**12**
Depth 2 (at least 3 upper level)	**12**

Electives

After you satisfy the specific degree requirements as listed above you can round out your degree with elective credits.

Arts and Sciences and Upper Level Requirements

60 of the total credits must be in the arts and sciences, at least 21 must be at the upper level. An additional 9 upper level credits may be earned in the applied professional area or arts and sciences.

STATUS REPORTS

In this section we will take a look at some Excelsior College Status Reports. There are two types of reports: unofficial reports given as part of the application and acceptance process, and official reports generated upon enrollment or matriculation to the college. The official status reports are updated periodically as you transfer your coursework or exams.

The status reports in this section are not necessarily the full report for a given student. Only sections were copied, but they are taken from actual reports issued to students. The idea of this section is to give you real world view and help you visualize how courses and exams fit into the degree program.

These reports are reproduced for illustrative purposes only.

Here we have a sample unofficial Excelsior College Status Report.

EXCELSIOR ⚕ COLLEGE℠

7 Columbia Circle, Albany NY 12203-5159
888-647-2388 / 518-464-8500
fax: 518-464-8777

Name:
Created:
Student ID:

Here is the section listing the transfer credits from an AARTS accredited yeshiva. As noted earlier in the section discussing yeshiva credits, students who completed a minimum of 45 credits from an Association for Advanced Rabbinical and Talmudic Schools (AARTS) accredited school will receive 30 lower-level credits in transfer. Notice how the courses are transcripted.

MESIVTA TORAH VODAATH RABBINICAL SEMINARY		Grade	Written English	Humanities	Social Science/History	Natural Science/Math	Applied Professional	Concentration	Core	Depth 1	Depth 2	Lab
2005/FA	HEBREW (TALMUDIC)	P		6.00								
2005/FA	YIDDISH (TALMUDIC)	P		3.00								
2005/FA	HEBREW LITERATURE	P		6.00								
2005/FA	CLASSICAL BIBLICAL PHILOSOPHY	P		3.00								
2005/FA	CLASSICAL BIBLICAL ETHICS	P		3.00								
2005/FA H	PUBLIC SPEAKING	P		3.00								
2005/FA	JEWISH HISTORY	P			6.00							

This student also took Judaic courses from AHS.

ASSOCIATION FOR HEBRAIC STUDIES INSTITUTE		Grade	Written English	Humanities	Social Science/History	Natural Science/Math	Applied Professional	Concentration	Core	Depth 1	Depth 2	Lab
BIBLICAL EXEGESIS: JOSHUA (BIB 205)												
2006/FA	JUDAIC STUDIES	P		3.00								
TALMUD: BAVA KAMA I												
2006/FA	JUDAIC STUDIES	P		6.00								
DIETARY LAWS II (JLW 431)												
2007/FA U	JUDAIC STUDIES	P					3.00					
BIBLICAL EXEGESIS: JUDGES (BIB 225)												
2007/FA	JUDAIC STUDIES	P		3.00								

He also took some CLEPs including College Algebra. Note that Excelsior will convert the score on select exams to a letter grade. Note also the "Q" before the exam title. This indicates this exam satisfied the quantitative/math requirement.

CLEP SUBJECT EXAMINATIONS			Grade	Written English	Humanities	Social Science/ History	Natural Science/ Math	Applied Professional	Concentration	Core	Depth 1	Depth 2	Lab
2006/06	Q	COLLEGE ALGEBRA (76)	A				3.00						

The report concludes with a record of the evaluations performed by the college mentors. Notice it lists the total number of credit hours and the totals for each of the three categories: Humanities, Social Sciences/History and Natural Sciences/Mathematics.

Historical Evaluation Listing

Eval Date	Eval Init	Eval GPA	Total Hours	Total Hrs Written English	Total Hrs Humanities	Total Hrs Social Science/ History	Total Hrs Natural Science Math	Total Hrs Upper Arts & Science	Total Hrs Applied Professional	Total Hrs Upper Applied Professional
		4.00	71.01	0.00	39.00	15.00	3.00	0.00	14.01	11.01

Sample 2

This student took AP exams while in high school.

ADVANCED PLACEMENT EXAMINATIONS			Grade	Written English	Humanities	Social Science/ History	Natural Science/ Math	Applied Professional	Concentration	Core	Depth 1	Depth 2	Lab
2003/FA		US HISTORY (5)	P			6.00							
2004/SP	#	ENG LIT/COMP (5)	P	3.00									
2004/SP		CALCULUS AB (5)	P				4.00						
2004/SP		PSYCHOLOGY (5)	P			3.00							
2004/SP		ENG LIT/COMP (5)	P		3.00								

The student also attended a seminary in Israel as part of a study abroad program. This allowed the student to transfer her credits as discussed earlier in the Study Abroad section.

HEBREW THEOLOGICAL COLLEGE			Grade	Written English	Humanities	Social Science/ History	Natural Science/ Math	Applied Professional	Concentration	Core	Depth 1	Depth 2	Lab
2004/FA	BIBL*111	THE PENTATEUCH WITH COMMENTARIES I	B		3.00								
2004/FA	BIBL*141	INTRODUCTION TO EARLY PROPHETS I	A		3.00								
2004/FA	BIBL*226	READINGS IN PROPHETS & HAGIOGRAPHA	B		2.00								
2004/FA	HIST*203	TOPICS IN CONTEMPORARY JEWISH HISTORY	B			2.00							
2004/FA	JLAW*101	INTRO TO JEWISH LIFE CYCLES I : CALENDAR	A					3.00					X
2004/FA	PHIL*130	SURVEY OF GREAT JEWISH THINKERS	A		2.00								
2005/SP	BIBL*112	THE PENTATEUCH WITH COMMENTARIES II	B		3.00								X
2005/SP	BIBL*142	INTRODUCTION TO EARLY PROPHETS II	A		3.00								X
2005/SP	HIST*132	HIST ANCIENT ISRAEL: 2ND COMMONWEALTH	A			2.00							
2005/SP	HIST*241	EVOLUTION OF THE ORAL LAW	B			2.00							
2005/SP	JLAW*102	INTRO TO JEWISH LIFE CYCLES II: FAMILY	A					3.00					X

She took the NYU exam and scored a perfect 16 points and had 16 credits granted in transfer. Notice that 12 are considered lower level and 4 are upper level.

NEW YORK UNIVERSITY			Grade	Written English	Humanities	Social Science/ History	Natural Science/ Math	Applied Professional	Concentration	Core	Depth 1	Depth 2	Lab
HEBREW													
2005/10 U		UPPER LEVEL	P		4.00					X			
2005/10		LOWER LEVEL	P		12.00					X			

She also took an Excelsior College course on Information Literacy. This course satisfies the information literacy requirement as noted by the "IL" designation in the "Core" column.

EXCELSIOR COLLEGE			Grade	Written English	Humanities	Social Science/ History	Natural Science/ Math	Applied Professional	Concentration	Core	Depth 1	Depth 2	Lab
2006/FA	INL*102	INFORMATION LITERACY	P					1.00		IL			

Here is a DSST exam.

DANTES SUBJECT STANDARDIZED TEST			Grade	Written English	Humanities	Social Science/History	Natural Science Math	Applied Professional	Concentration	Core	Depth 1	Depth 2	Lab
2006/08	SH*532	PRINCIPLES OF SUPERVISION (53)	A					3.00					
2006/08	SG*511	ENVIRONMENT AND HUMANITY: THE RACE TO SAVE THE PLANET (53)	B				3.00						

Once again take a look at the evaluation summary. Notice how all the credits are tallied in their respective categories.

Eval Date	Eval Init	Eval GPA	Total Hours	Total Hrs Written English	Total Hrs Humanities	Total Hrs Social Science/ History	Total Hrs Natural Science Math	Total Hrs Upper Arts & Science	Total Hrs Applied Professional	Total Hrs Upper Applied Professional
12/18/07	KM	3.58	108.00	3.00	43.00	24.00	19.00	4.00	19.00	9.00

Section 8

ACCREDITATION

Not Kosher!

ACCREDITATION

In the United States, accreditation is carried out by private organizations and not governmental bodies. An exception may be the NYS Department of Education, which does accredit colleges. This is very different from Europe, where accreditation is generally a governmental affair carried out by the Ministry of Education in a specific country.

There are three different types of accrediting organizations: regional accreditation, national accreditation and specialized accreditation. While, in theory, one level of accreditation should not be more accepted than another, the reality may be quite different. Many consider regional accreditation as the gold standard. If you look through college catalogs or websites of regionally accredited colleges, you may find statements on the acceptance of transfer credits. Many list regional accreditation as the initial requirement. However, it is important to keep in mind that acceptance of transfer credit is up to the receiving institution. Also, many times what is written regarding transfer credit acceptance is often not written in stone. Therefore, if you have credits from another college that is not regionally accredited, don't discount them. It may pay to ask and then go up the chain of command

In this guide, we won't go through the whole shebang, just what we will call "accreditation al regel achas."

Keep in mind that just because a school is not accredited does not mean it is not legitimate and doesn't offer a quality program. Generally speaking, all schools start out as unaccredited as most accrediting bodies require a school to be in operation for a minimum amount of time before being eligible to apply for accreditation.
ED.GOV

if you initially do not get the response you are looking for.

Getting back to the U.S. system of accreditation: if the government does not offer accreditation and we rely on private organizations, who "accredits" the accreditors? That's a good question. Briefly, there are two organizations which recognize the accreditors: The U.S. Department of Education (USDE), which is federal, and the Council for Higher Education Accreditation (CHEA), which is private and made up of a board of directors.

When selecting a college, be sure to check that the college is accredited and if so, by which entity. Make sure the accreditor is legitimate and recognized by the USDE, CHEA or both, and be sure that the type of accreditation will suit your purposes.

"Diploma Mill"
An institution of higher education operating without supervision of a state or professional agency and granting diplomas which are either fraudulent or, because of the lack of proper standards, worthless.

WEBSTER'S THIRD NEW INTERNATIONAL

DICTIONARY

Students beware! You may notice that most colleges have a web address that ends in .edu. However, not all institutions that use .edu as a part of their Internet address are legitimate. Before the U.S. Department of Commerce created its current, strict requirements, some questionable institutions were approved to use a .edu. The current requirements allow only colleges and institutions accredited by an agency recognized by the U.S. Department of Education to use the .edu. However, some more suspect institutions have maintained the .edu addresses. Don't judge an institution by its web address.

ED.GOV

PLAGIARISM

A true story; believe it or not.

PLAGIARISM

One of the major issues of concern in education in general is plagiarism. This is where one expresses someone else's idea as his own. Plagiarism is not just buying a term paper and submitting it as your own. Plagiarism may even occur with just a few lines of text in an assignment that is otherwise all your own work. Here are some tips taken from a Charter Oak State College newsletter which were adapted from the Writing Tutorial Services, Indiana University website June 11, 2004. http://www.indiana.edu/~wts/wts/plagiarism.html.

"You must give credit whenever you use:

⚜ Another person's ideas, words, opinion, or theory

⚜ Any facts, statistics, graphs, drawings—any pieces of information—that are not common knowledge

⚜ Quotations of another person's written or spoken words or

⚜ Paraphrase another person's spoken or written words."

Remember—*"using another person's phrases or sentences without putting quotation marks around them is considered plagiarism even if the writer cites in her own text*

Lehavdil ben kodesh l'chol, we find a similar idea throughout the Talmud. In many passages in the Talmud we have a long list of who said a certain teaching in the name of whom. The Talmudic sage, Rav Elazar, said in the name of Rav Chanina; "Whoever repeats a saying in the name of its originator brings deliverance to the world, as it says in Megillas Esther, 'And Esther told the king in the name of Mordechai.'"

This reminds me of a story told over about the Chasam Sofer. One of his talmidim reported that he was visiting another area, and the Rabbi, during a drasha, was discussing ideas that originated from the Chasam Sofer but the Rabbi did not give the Chasam Sofer credit. Whereupon the Chasam Sofer responded, "Saying over my Torah in his own name is fine, as long as he doesn't say over his Torah in my name."

the source of the phrase or sentences she has quoted."

(from Writing Tutorial Services, Indiana University website June 11, 2004—**http://www. indiana.edu/~wts/wts/plagiarism.html**)

You must give credit where credit is due. While it may be true that you did not mean to plagiarize, the bottom line is that your instructor generally cannot read minds and doesn't know whether you plagiarized intentionally or not. Plagiarism will generally result in an "F" for the courses and may also lead to suspension or dismissal from the college. The bottom line is: give credit where credit is due. It may be true that *"imitation is the sincerest form of flattery."* However, you must credit another person's work.

There are really three reasons for citing sources:

+ Fairness and honesty: to identify materials and information not your own; to avoid plagiarism (even unintentional).
+ Authenticity and authority: to support your ideas with the research and opinions of experts.
+ Confirmation and retrieval: to allow readers to locate your sources for confirmation of what you've said or to learn more about the topic.

Maryanne LeGrow, Ph.D., Charter Oak State College

Section 10

CERTIFICATE PROGRAMS

Charter Oak State College

Excelsior College

Louisiana State University

Thomas Edison State College

Congratulations!...
You're certifiable.

CERTIFICATE PROGRAMS—NON-DEGREE STUDIES

While this book is primarily about how to earn your degree, a degree program may not be appropriate for every student. For some, it may be about academics: for others, it may be about time or money or the lack thereof. Whatever the reason, this does not mean their education must stop at a high school diploma. Many students go on to earn certificates or diplomas in various fields or areas of interest. Some may tend to be theoretically oriented, while others are vocational. Many colleges offer certificate programs. Additionally, there are many non-degree granting institutions offering certificate programs or courses.

Many certificates offered by colleges are composed of a specific series of standard, for-credit college courses. The benefit of having a certificate made up of credit bearing courses is that it will likely be much easier to use those courses toward a college degree, should you choose to do so in the future. Otherwise, you may have to go through the prior learning assessment or portfolio process to have those courses recognized as the equivalent of college level (credit-bearing) courses. Some non-degree granting institutions have their courses evaluated by the American Council of Education or National PONSI for credit recommendations. These credit recommendations may significantly ease the credit transfer process should you choose to move on to earning a degree.

Please keep in mind that certificate programs are not only for students not interested in a degree. In fact, many degree seeking students, or students who already have a degree, choose to enroll in certificate programs to enhance their knowledge in a specific area and/or earn a credential to demonstrate expertise in a given area.

Listed here is just a small sampling of available college credit certificate programs.

CHARTER OAK STATE COLLEGE CERTIFICATE PROGRAMS

The Charter Oak certificate programs are designed for adults who are interested in learning a specific set of skills and gaining knowledge in a certain area, but may not want to earn a degree. Credits earned apply toward a Charter Oak associate or baccalaureate degree. The following certificate courses are all offered online, in accelerated, convenient, 5- or 8-week terms. Students do not even need to be matriculated with the college.

- After School Education Certificate
- Computer Security Certificate
- Health Insurance Customer Service Certificate
- Paralegal Certificate
- Project Management Certificate
- Public Safety Certificate

Charter Oak State College

55 Paul J. Manafort Drive

New Britain, CT 06053-2150

860.832.3800

info@charteroak.edu

www.charteroak.edu

EXCELSIOR COLLEGE

Excelsior College offers several certificate programs. Certificates require 5 courses. These courses are available online from Excelsior. Credits earned can also be applied to Excelsior college degree programs.

- Certificate in Entrepreneurship
- Homeland Security Certificate

Health Care certificates are available too.

Excelsior College

7 Columbia Circle

Albany, NY 12203-5159

(888) 647-2388

(518) 464-8500

admissions@excelsior.edu

www.excelsior.edu

LOUISIANA STATE UNIVERSITY CONTINUING EDUCATION CERTIFICATE PROGRAMS

Louisiana State University offers several undergraduate credit certificates. Each program consists of five courses totaling 15 semester credit hours. In each program there are four required courses and one elective course.

- Certificate of Liberal Studies
- Business Communication Certificate
- Human Services Certificate

LSU Independent and Distance Learning

1227 Pleasant Hall, LSU

Baton Rouge, LA 70803

225-578-3920

800-234-5046

iscreditcertificate@doce.lsu.edu

www.is.lsu.edu

THOMAS EDISON STATE COLLEGE

Undergraduate certificates are 18-credit programs that provide students with a solid foundation in a chosen area of study, or major, and are designed to transfer easily into a degree program at Thomas Edison State College. Students may select from the following undergraduate certificate programs:

- Undergraduate Certificate in Accounting
- Undergraduate Certificate in Computer-Aided Design
- Undergraduate Certificate in Computer Information Systems
- Undergraduate Certificate in Computer Science
- Undergraduate Certificate in E-Commerce (12 credit program)
- Undergraduate Certificate in Electronics
- Undergraduate Certificate in Finance
- Undergraduate Certificate in Fitness and Wellness Services
- Undergraduate Certificate in Human Resources Management
- Undergraduate Certificate in Labor Studies
- Undergraduate Certificate in Marketing
- Undergraduate Certificate in Operations Management
- Undergraduate Certificate in Public Administration

Thomas Edison State College
101 W. State Street
Trenton, NJ 08608-1176
(609) 984-1164
(888) 442-8372
info@tesc.edu
www.tesc.edu

Section 11

COMMUNITY PROGRAMS

AHS Institute

COPE Institute

The New Seminary

Institute for Special Education of Sara Schenirer

Testing and Training International/TTI

Maalot/Zaidner Institute

Maalot Los Angeles

Young Israel Educational Programs

COMMUNITY PROGRAMS

In this section, we introduce you to a variety of educational programs available to the Jewish community. This includes certificate, undergraduate and graduate offerings seeking to serve various segments of the Jewish community. Only some of these programs offer courses by distance learning or credit-by-exam. Several organizations offer degree programs in conjunction with the college granting the degree, where the college faculty teaches courses at the organizations' location within the community.

AHS INSTITUTE

251 Grandview Avenue
Suffern, NY 10901
Tel: 888-259-4374
Tel: 845-362-6954
Fax: 877-329-0247
info@ahsinstitute.org
www.ahsinstitute.org

The Association for Hebraic Studies—AHS Institute was established to provide students with coursework in Hebraic/Judaic studies. AHS offers courses in the traditional classroom format, as well as through distance learning and independent study.

The curriculum is designed to give students both a broad and in-depth view in areas of Judaic studies. Theoretical and practical applications are stressed, and emphasis is placed on using the traditional texts and original sources. The curriculum is designed to articulate with degree programs offered at regionally accredited colleges and universities. Students combine their general education courses, professional courses and AHS courses to complete their associate or baccalaureate degrees at institutions of higher education.

AHS Institute, in cooperation with Charter Oak State College, Excelsior College, and others, provides students with the opportunity to earn a regionally accredited degree without attending the traditional college campus.

Students can earn a regionally accredited degree by combining AHS courses, traditional and distance learning college courses, and approved college level exams. The exact number of AHS courses applicable towards a degree will vary depending on the college and a student's field of study.

AHS Institute offers courses or exams in Tanach, Talmud, Jewish Thought, Ethics, Bioethics, Business Ethics, Halacha, and Jewish History.

AHS students are men and women from across the U.S., Canada and Israel. They are graduates from a range of *Yeshivas, Bais Yaakov,s* and seminaries. Some are working and others are still in yeshiva or seminary. The key to the successful AHS student is motivation. Students take AHS courses at various stages in their degree program. Some students need only one course to graduate, while others take ten or more courses.

COPE INSTITUTE

225 Broadway
New York, NY 10007
Tel: 212-809-5935
Fax: 212-809-4132

Junior Accounting/Assistant Controller program
COPE Institute, a division of Agudath Israel of America, is a NYS registered business school and accredited by Accrediting Council for Independent Colleges and Schools. They offer a Junior Accounting/Assistant Controller program. The courses in this program are recommended for 21 college credits by ACE.

COPE offers students this intensive accounting program in Brooklyn and Manhattan. There are separate classes for men and women. The men's program is offered during the day in downtown Manhattan. Day and evening classes are offered for women in Boro Park. COPE also offers students the opportunity to continue their education and earn a BS in Accounting/NYS CPA Track, through Excelsior College with their CPA track program, at their Brooklyn location.

THE NEW SEMINARY

2600 Ocean Avenue

Brooklyn, NY 11229

Tel: 718-769-8160

Fax: 718-769-8640

Bachelor's degree programs (various fields)

BS in Nursing

Occupational Therapy

Master's in Education

Master of Social Work

The New Seminary, also known as Rebbetzin Bulka's Seminary, offers a variety of degree programs, for women. The undergraduate programs, offered in conjunction with Adelphi University, allow students to earn credits for *limudei kodesh* courses. Seminary courses are offered in Brooklyn and Monsey. Secular courses are taught by Adelphi faculty at The New Seminary in Brooklyn. Students earn a bachelor's degree that can prepare them for several different fields. They also offer a BS in Nursing that can be completed in two and a half years. Students in the Master's in Education also have the opportunity to earn an optional Advanced Certificate in Graduate Studies- focusing on Special Education or Literacy. A Master of Social Work is being offered in 2008 in conjunction with Long Island University.

INSTITUTE FOR SPECIAL EDUCATION OF SARA SCHENIRER

4622 14th Avenue
Brooklyn, NY 11219
Tel: 718-633-8557

Bachelor's in Behavioral Science
Master's in Education
> Early Childhood
> Elementary Education
> Special Education

The Institute for Special Education, better known as Sara Schenirer, specializes in training women teachers. The undergraduate and graduate programs are offered in conjunction with Mercy College. The Bachelor's degree can be earned in as little as one year. Credits are earned through courses given at the Institute as well as transfer from seminary and prior learning assessment. The Master's program affords students the opportunity to earn teaching certification in a number of areas. Classes are offered in Brooklyn and Monsey. Plans are in place to offer the Master's in Lakewood for students who have graduated the Institute undergraduate program. The Institute has recently started and Adult Education Division to accommodate older students who have been out of school for some time.

TESTING AND TRAINING INTERNATIONAL—TTI

Tel: 877-RING-TTI; Tel: 718-376-0974
TTI advises students on completing nontraditional undergraduate programs. They also serve as a test center for various credit by exam programs, including CLEP, and also offer a series of Jewish Studies examinations that can be transferred for credit. TTI maintains a lending library of study aids to help students prepare for examinations.

Graduate programs in Occupational Therapy, School Counseling, Special Education and Speech Pathology are offered by TTI, in conjunction with various colleges. Graduate programs are offered onsite at locations in Brooklyn, Monsey, Lakewood, and Israel. Additional graduate programs may be added in the future.

MAALOT/ZAIDNER INSTITUTE

P.O. Box 43016 Beit Yitzchak Street
Har Nof, Jerusalem
Tel: 972-2-654-4549
Fax: 972-2-651-9376
http://www.nevey.org/maalotb.htm

Maalot Yerushalayim and its branches provide a college-level education. Besides for locations in Israel, there are branches in New York, Baltimore, England, Montreal, Detroit, and Los Angeles. Some programs are also available in Yeshivas for men. Many Neve affiliated seminaries also offer Maalot coursework.

The mission of the program is to provide men and women with the opportunity to pursue advanced Jewish studies, while at the same time achieving a level of secular education enabling entry into the job markets of Israel the United States, and Europe. Maalot also seeks to meet the needs of men and women who must balance their desire for educationally valid study with family obligations.

Maalot offers courses in Judaic Studies and several other fields including, Computers, Business, Graphic Arts, Speech Pathology, and Education/Psychology. Not all courses are available at all branches. Courses are classroom-based. Evening and part-time studies may be offered at some branches. For admission and other information, students should directly contact the branch they are seeking to attend.

Maalot courses carry credit recommendations from ACE (American Council on Education) and the programs were developed to articulate with degree programs offered at Thomas Edison State College of New Jersey. Students seeking to transfer to other colleges should be aware that the acceptance of credits is up to the receiving institution.

MAALOT LOS ANGELES

Women: 323-938-5196, info@maalotla.org
Men: Yeshiva Educational Services, 323-633-0874, rdjla@msn.com

MA in Education: Curriculum and Instruction
MA in Special Education with Credential

Maalot of Los Angeles, a branch of Zaidner/Maalot in Israel, offers two on-line Master's degrees in Education. These programs are offered to qualified men and women from anywhere they have an internet connection. The MA in Education is offered through California State Bakersfield. The MA in Special Education is offered through Grand Canyon University in Arizona

YOUNG ISRAEL EDUCATIONAL PROGRAMS

111 John Street, Suite 450
New York, NY 10038
Tel: 212-929-1525 x115
masters@youngisrael.org
www.youngisrael.com

Master of Arts in Educational Leadership
Master of Business Administration

The Master of Arts builds on the training you already have. Through a unique partnership with Young Israel Educational Programs, Inc., Bellevue University accepts bachelor's degrees from any regionally accredited or Association of Advanced Rabbinical and Talmudic Schools accredited or affiliated institution. Bellevue University also awards as many as 6 credit hours for past college courses, rabbinic training and life experience. These credits can be applied toward a 36 credit hour Master of Arts Degree in Educational Leadership. Awarded college credits must be earned at a graduate level.

Bellevue University's Master of Arts combines theory and philosophy with real-life application. The Master of Arts program utilizes an adult-learning format, and is comprised of courses that encourage individual thought, synthesis of group contribution, and assimilation of practical and theoretical teachings. Its mission is to combine philosophy with real-life application of those concepts and theoretical models. In the Master of Arts program all students take a core group of leadership courses, delving into the subject of leadership, examining it from numerous perspectives. In addition, the student will take additional courses in the field of education to enhance their education and skills.

Depending on demand, an MBA, and an MA in Educational Leadership with Judaic Concentrations, are also offered.

All programs include a combination of on-site and online courses. Two intensive four-day onsite sessions are required and offered in NYC during the summers. All other courses are offered online. Government student loans are available.

Section 12

MORE... MEET THE STUDENTS

Meet Yocheved

I was interested in a speech therapy program but didn't want to attend any local college campus-based program. I wanted to choose the atmosphere that suited me, so I decided to go with distance learning. I heard about SKRG, an organization that helps advise students on distance learning programs, and they helped me plan my degree and made sure that I would have all the necessary prerequisite courses to enter a master's program in speech and language pathology.

The credits used toward my degree were an eclectic bunch. I had credits from my high school college program and seminary. After returning from seminary in Israel I earned credits from CLEP and DSST exams, the NYU Hebrew exam, and online courses in speech pathology from Red Rocks Community College in Colorado. I also took online courses from University of Alaska, which were used to satisfy some prerequisites for my masters but were not accepted for credit toward my undergraduate degree since they were continuing education courses and not college credit courses.

I enjoyed the online courses, felt I learned something and found them to be very convenient in terms of flexibility. I had deadlines but chose when and where to study. I compared some of the courses to those taken by friends in an on-campus course; while it seemed I had more work to complete, I preferred the convenience of the online courses over sitting in a classroom.

The most important factor when it came to the CLEP and DSST exams was motivation. I took my exams at the end of my degree program, so just knowing that when I finish these exams I'm done was motivation enough.

Meet Yocheved, continued

I definitely recommend distance learning; for me it was a very good experience. Everyone has to evaluate for themselves if they can do it. However, I think most people underestimate their abilities and could successfully complete their degree using distance learning. If you're on top of work and stick to a schedule it is very doable.

I enjoyed dealing with Charter Oak very much. As with all colleges, things take a long time to be processed; when dealing with them you need to allow yourself enough time! Whenever I needed anything from them, I called my advisor and she was extremely helpful and nice. She told me everything I needed to know and it was very easy to get in touch with her.

Yocheved earned a Bachelor's of Science in Liberal Studies from Charter Oak State College and received the Doris G. Cassiday Award. She recently moved to Israel and is slated to begin a Master's in Speech Pathology from the University of Cincinnati in conjunction with TTI.

In 9th grade, after taking the biology regents exam, I took out an AP biology book from the library and passed the Biology CLEP. In 10th grade, after taking a course for the Global Studies Regents, I took the Western Civilization I CLEP. (A friend of mine took Western Civilization II and passed.) I also took the General Math CLEP. In 11th grade, I took the Accounting CLEP; this was after I had two years of accounting courses. I also took the American History CLEP after taking the American History and Government Regents.

T. L. Monsey, NY

Meet Liba

I wanted to work full time while completing my degree but also knew that night classes were not available locally. I also wanted set my own pace and complete my degree faster than a traditional degree program would allow. I came back from seminary in Israel in June and finished my degree nine months later. Granted, I had 30 credits from college courses offered in high school and an additional thirty or so credits from seminary through a study abroad program. I had to get it done for my job.

I took a few CLEPs and about 10 or so AHS Judaic distance learning courses as well. I also took an online course from Excelsior college and information technology. I was very motivated to complete my degree and set goals and deadlines for myself. I would come home from work, relax, close the door to my room and study. While I set goals and made sure to stick to my deadlines, I made sure to set realistic goals and not overburden myself. I would be sure to reward myself, go for walks at night and have fun too.

The AHS courses were enjoyable. I learned a lot, the courses were comprehensive, and helped me focus on my learning. The exams were challenging but fair. If you studied you did well.

I definitely recommend nontraditional education to others. However, if you are using college credits in order to be able to move up the salary scale, be sure that your employer will recognize distance learning or credit by exam for salary increases. One of the public schools where I worked did not recognize credits earned through distance learning or exams for salary increases. However, they did recognize the completed nontraditional degree.

The staff and advisors at Excelsior College were very helpful, and always understanding with any issues that came up.

Meet Liba, continued

Liba earned a Bachelor's of Science degree in Liberal Arts from Excelsior College. She is currently enrolled in a Master's of Special Education online through Saint Leo University in Florida.

Meet Shmuel

> *I took a foreign language examination in Hebrew through the ACTFL. It's a phone interview and they provide testing in over 50 languages, some of which are recommended by ACE for college credit and accepted by Excelsior College. An advanced speaker of Hebrew will get six lower-level credits and six upper-level credits.*

Shmuel from the Mid-West

The ACTFL (American Council on the Teaching of Foreign Languages) Testing Program is administered by Language Testing International (LTI). Additional information can be obtained on the web at www.languagetesting.com or by calling 914-963-7110. The ACTFL oral proficiency tests that are recommended for college credit are accepted by Charter Oak State College and Excelsior College.

Melech's Exam Experience

I took English Composition with Essay, a must for those who don't want to a sit through a semester writing until their hands fall off. It's challenging to try to write an essay in 45 minutes, but those grading the essay know that, and the main thing is to use a CLEP book to prac-tice the grammar. Do the problems once, try to review the ones you got wrong and understand why they are wrong, and then do the prob-lems a day before the test. After reading the essay question, spend a few minutes trying to come up with a mental and/or written generic outline of what you're going to write, and then just keep typing. If the beginning of what you write looks good, even if you run out of time be-fore being able to write your concluding paragraph, I don't think you'll lose too many points. Hard to know though, since I don't have a clue what cost me points when I took it.

I used the Barron's NYS Regents American History book to prepare for the US History II CLEP, and my guess is that it's probably of little use for the US History I CLEP. Far more detail is given for post- than for pre- civil war America. Use it as your primary text, and try to make sure you can answer the questions after each section, and then read the REA book after each unit. The CLEP questions will be most similar to what you see in the REA book, but I personally think it better to use it as a supplementary text after the Barron's. Take the two or three practice CLEPs in the REA CD within a couple days before the test, but make sure you're pretty prepared beforehand. Make sure to review wrong answers (consider re-reading the entire paragraph in the REA book in which the answer appears) before moving on to the next test.

Melech's Exam Experience, continued

I took a sociology CLEP, using a very fact intensive Cliff Notes as my primary source, and REA as a secondary source, in a similar fashion. You can certainly teach yourself sociology, but it definitely requires a lot of time. Take the practice tests in the same way.

M.B. Ohio

Meet Miriam

By the time I decided to finish up my degree I already had two kids and was working part-time and did not have the time to attend a traditional degree program. I also wanted to utilize all the Judaic credits that I already earned.

I earned a Bachelors of Science degree with a concentration in Judaic Studies from Charter Oak State College. Charter Oak was very helpful; they were always available and accommodating, allowing me to take a leave of absence when necessary. They were extremely helpful in planning my degree, allowing me to make the most of the credits already earned.

Miriam earned credits through her high school college program, a couple of exams taken while in high school, seminary and a few traditional college courses. She finally completed her degree after she learned about AHS and realized all she needed was a few more courses in Judaic Studies to earn a degree with a concentration in Judaic Studies. Miriam is currently a cardiac ultrasound technician in New York.

Meet Chaim

Charter Oak State College and AHS Institute afforded me the opportunity to finish my degree at my own leisure, while focusing on my yeshiva learning. The Charter Oak degree program was flexible and allowed me to design my own concentration, which would maximize my existing credits and help for my future career goals.

I don't consider myself the most motivated or studious person; however, I knew I had to finish and that was motivation enough. A mature person should realize the importance of his education for future opportunities and planned career.

A nontraditional degree program is a sensible choice. It gives you the opportunity for a college education on your own terms; you decide how to earn the credits, through online or classroom courses, or exams. It gave me the opportunity to stay in yeshiva and set my own pace. The Judaic courses I took from AHS Institute gave me the opportunity to earn credit for some of what I was learning in yeshiva and also explore other subjects such as Jewish history.

My experience with Charter Oak was very pleasant. From my academic advisor to the people in the business office, everyone was helpful.

Chaim is finishing up his last two classes toward a Bachelor's of Science in Liberal Studies at Charter Oak State College. He is teaching in the Five Towns and is already admitted to a Master's of Education program in NYC.

Aviva's Exam Experience

Sociology—I found it to be very easy to get a high score. I was told that all I needed to do was to get a regular sociology textbook and become familiar with the definitions in the back, since most sociology concepts are common sense—it is only the terminology that is new. This probably takes reading a bit every night for a week. Personally, I thought it was interesting so I skimmed through the textbook quickly as well. I took it in the summer before twelfth grade.

Psychology—I studied a good deal. I used a Psych AP book because I could not find a Psych CLEP study guide. I studied the book as a CLEP period for 45 minutes twice a week for as long as the regular Psych class met. The advantage was that the regular class spent an hour and a half twice a week, and I always started my CLEP period about ten minutes late. I didn't have time take the CLEP until a month after I stopped studying, so I then skimmed it again to refresh my memory over the course of two days. I took it in January of twelfth grade.

Computers—I got the lowest score of the three, but that's because I didn't study from a book. I just looked over the notes my friend took while studying for the CLEP. The test was quite easy; if I had skimmed through a book I would have been fine. Some of it was basic computer knowledge but there was plenty about networking and other topics that a Word processor may never hear of.

A.B. Monsey

Baila's Exam Experience

For someone who is motivated, wants to save money, and is able to do independent study, CLEPing is the way to go!!! Here's a tip: before you decide on taking CLEP, make sure it is something that will go towards your degree, meaning that you actually need those specific credits; also some colleges don't accept CLEPs. There are a bunch of CLEPs to take in all areas of study. Here's a list of the ones that I took and what I thought of them:

1. Analyzing and Interpreting Literature—6 credits.
This was pretty straightforward. I took it straight out of high school while I was still in SAT and literature mode...I got a CLEP book out of the library and I think I studied for a couple of days, for a few hours each day. I went through the practice tests and then I WENT FOR IT I passed! There are plenty of people who don't even study. I highly recommend this CLEP.

2. English Composition with Essay—6 credits.
This also has a writing skills component and you have to write an essay. I went according to a CLEP book and spent about a week practicing essays that I had someone critique for me. It went well!

3. Human Growth and Development—3 credits.
The concepts are pretty basic, things that most people already know. It's basically getting the terminology straight. I studied for a couple of weeks, took the practice tests, and used one of the online programs that help you study. I found the test relatively straightforward. (Make sure to know the names and the different theories!)

Baila's Exam Experience, continued

4. Educational Psychology—3 credits.

I know a lot of people who take this CLEP on the same day as the Human Growth and Development CLEP. However I felt that one success was enough for one day, so I went home and studied a little more (found some info for the CLEP online that helped me a little) and I took the CLEP a week later. It was pretty logical concepts and overlapped with the Human Growth and Development CLEP content.

* Though I didn't take it, I know a number of girls who took the College Mathematics CLEP right after their high school math final. They studied a bit more, learned a little more new material and they were able to earn 6 credits for something that would be much harder 3 years later starting all over...

Baila shares some of her thoughts on several exams. In doing so, she also brings up some good tips. A) Take an exam when you're in the thick of the subject matter. In other words, if you are studying literature, look for exams in that area. She capitalized on her preparation for the SAT and high school English/literature classes and supplemented it with some additional study and took the Analyzing and Interpreting Literature exam. B) Writing is an important skill. I believe the best way to learn to write is to, well, write! Prepare some essays and give it to others to critique. C) If you have an interest in a subject or are studying for an exam, look and see if there are others that may be closely related. Several students have suggested studying for certain exams together or one after another. Among those suggestions was to prepare for Intro to Psychology, Human Growth and Development and Educational Psychology in succession. D) Last but not least, take the time to study.

AFTERWORD

AFTERWORD

If you've reached this point congratulations are in order, assuming, of course, that you read from the beginning of this book and didn't just skip to the end. It is my hope that after reading this guide for the first time, you have gained a basic understanding of non-traditional education and the tools to help you begin planning your degree.

As the writing of this book was coming to a close, I had an interesting thought: it would be interesting if this book could serve as the basis for a credit-bearing educational planning course for a non-traditional college degree. This is, in fact, currently in the planning stage.

Allow me to suggest the following. After completing an initial reading of this book, take some time to request literature from the various testing programs and institutions from which you may wish to earn credits, or view the information on their websites. While it is true that this piece of advice seems to belong in the introduction, I didn't want to scare you off by assigning homework from the start. Remember, this book wasn't meant to replace the "official" literature and information provided by the colleges or organizations discussed; it is here to supplement it and guide you through the process, focusing on the interests and sensitivities of our audience.

Students: take an active role in planning your education. Parents: it's okay to help your child plan for his or her education. However, be sure to involve your child; he or she is the student and should learn about the process. Many times parents call me to help advise them on their child's education. Inevitably I end up having the same conversation with the student. The colleges are also wary of having parents call on behalf of their child. Remember, you are dealing with nontraditional colleges offering nontraditional degree programs. To succeed, students must be mature, independent, and motivated. It's okay for a parent to make the initial call, but be sure to involve the student as well.

Whether you are still in high school or have grandchildren in high school, non-traditional education is a wonderful option. For the most part, in our community it seems that non-traditional degree options are associated with high school students, those in seminary and perhaps those a few years post *Beis Medrash*. However, if you look at the statistics of the general student body at Charter Oak State College, Excelsior College, and Thomas Edison State College, the average age may surprise you: it ranges from 35 to 41. Excelsior reports that for the class of 2007, the oldest graduate was an 82-year-old woman from California who earned a Master of Arts in Liberal Studies. She also earned an associate degree from Excelsior in 1986. The youngest graduate was an 18-year-old woman from Brooklyn, NY who earned a Bachelor of Science in Liberal Arts. At Charter Oak, graduates ranged in age from 19 to 67. So you see it is never too early or too late to start planning for your degree. Now that you know the average age of the students at these schools, you can imagine why such schools may be wary of only dealing with parents of the students and not the students themselves.

Even if you are not sure that you wish to eventually earn a degree, consider your options in terms of earning credit NOW. It may save you a lot of time and money. Many Bais Yaakov high school girls in ninth grade and up end up taking CLEP exams which correspond to what they may have learned during the school year. In New York especially, where high school students take the New York State Regents Examinations, the State's standardized exams, I counsel students to review the CLEP exam outlines for the corresponding subjects of the course they have taken. Many find that with little or no extra studying they are able to complete and satisfactorily pass the CLEP examination in that subject. Generally speaking, you want the students, especially younger students, to take an exam, especially their first exam, in a subject they are familiar with and feel comfortable that they will pass. Otherwise, if they fail, they may lose confidence in their ability to use the credit by examination approach. This year, following the Biology Regents exam, I spoke with several students who attempted to take the CLEP examination in biology, which is recommended for six credits, to see how they fared. While the results of my informal survey may seem disappointing as approximately 40% of the students failed this exam, upon discussing their study approach and preparations for this CLEP exam, most of the students who failed did not bother preparing for the CLEP examination; they basically relied solely on the preparation that they put into the Regents biology exam. While those students may have done well on the biology exam, the topics covered on the Regents exam is not representative of the topics of the CLEP exam. Many of the students who passed the CLEP did spend some time using a CLEP study guide, in the days following the Regents exam. Therefore, if you are a parent encouraging your son or daughter to take the CLEP examinations, encourage them to brush up. Also be prepared to boost their morale in case they do not do as well as they expected. This approach can work for a high school course that has a corresponding subject in the CLEP or other examination program. I only chose to illustrate this with Regents courses since I find that the Regents exams provide an additional impetus for students to study.

If you have any questions or comments please visit the publisher's website to send a message or use fax or mail to contact me. Please let me know if you found this book helpful. I also look forward to constructive criticism. Don't forget to share your experiences so it can be included on the website or future editions of this book. I really mean it. Please share your educational journey experiences.

When I began writing this book the idea was to produce a short pamphlet on the degree process, a couple of pages at most. However, as I began to write, sections were added. Whenever I thought the end was near additional sections were added or existing ones expanded. There was no end in sight. A decision had to be made when the time came to close the book. A revised edition can be produced in the future if and when it is needed. As this book was undergoing final editing, I was speaking with a colleague at a non-traditional college. I mentioned that one of my reasons for writing this book was due to time constraints; it is difficult to find the time to speak to every person looking for direction and explain the degree process. I figured that by putting it down on paper a lot of questions would be answered, and while some new questions may arise in the long run, students will be more familiar with the degree process and some time will be saved. He responded, and I paraphrase, *"The problem is you're writing a book and not a pamphlet. Students call the admissions office at the college or their advisors and don't bother reading any of the College's publications."* It is my hope that I succeeded in preparing a book—and not a pamphlet—that is an enjoyable read and that is, in fact, read.

Wishing you much *Hatzlocha* on your educational endeavor.

Section 14

APPENDIX

Liberal Arts

Exam List for Charter Oak State College

Charter Oak Capstone

Exam List for Excelsior College

Accrediting Agencies

Distance Education & Training Council/DETC

Empire State College

Thomas Edison State College/TESC

Contacts & Resources

College: *Issur Cheftza* or *Gavra*?

Appendix ap.pen.dix ə-pĕn'dĭks

Anatomy: A part of the body whose purpose remains a mystery.

Publication: A part of the book we stuff material we don't know what else to do with.

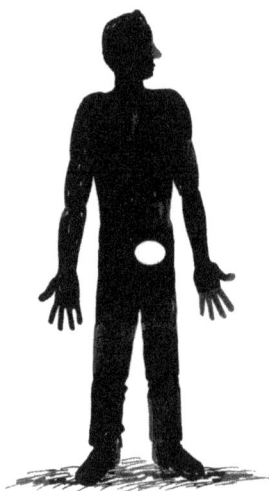

APPENDIX A: LIBERAL ARTS

The following lists are adapted from Charter Oak State College publications, and listed here to help you identify courses or disciplines that may be classified as liberal arts, or arts and sciences.

Humanities
Art
Advanced Writing
Communication
Dance
Film
Foreign Languages
Journalism
Literature
Music
Philosophy
Photography
Religion
Speech
Theater

Natural Sciences & Mathematics
Astronomy
Biology
Chemistry
Environmental Sciences
Geology
Mathematics
Meteorology
Physics

Social Sciences
Anthropology
Archaeology
Economics
Geography
History
Political Science
Psychology
Sociology

Examples of Courses That Do NOT Meet Liberal Arts Requirements

Accounting	Insurance
Allied Health	Library Science
Aviation	Management of Human Resources
Business Law	Marketing
Data Processing	Nursing
Education	Operations Management
Electronics	Radiologic Technology
Engineering/Engineering Technology	Real Estate
Finance	Recreation
Fire Science	Rehabilitation Services
Health Education	Secretarial Science
Health Services	Social Work
Home Economics	Technical Services

PLEASE NOTE: These lists are provided only as a guide. They do not represent all liberal arts courses, nor do they ensure that every course listed will be assigned as such.

APPENDIX B: EXAM LIST FOR CHARTER OAK STATE COLLEGE

These requirements are for students who matriculated (enrolled) after July 1, 2005.

Key to General Education

Students who matriculated on or after July 1, 2005	
a	Literature
b	Behavioral/Social Science
d	Ethical Decision Making
e	Written Communication
g	Global Understanding
q	Mathematics
n	Non U.S. History/Culture
o	Oral Communication
s	Natural Science
u	U.S. History/Government
y	Information Literacy

NOTE: Some comprehensive examinations may yield credit in more than one subject and/or subject area. Information on these credit values will be provided upon request by subject area, for all comprehensive examinations. Charter Oak accepts some tests as lower level even though ACE or the testing agency recommends upper level.

Exams Accepted by Charter Oak State College (As of December 2008)
The following list was taken from the Charter Oak website.

Examination	Testing Program	Minimum Req'd Score	Credits	Level	General Ed	Liberal Arts
ANTHROPOLOGY						
General Anthropology	DSST/DANTES	47	3	L	b	Yes
ART						
Art of the Western World	DSST/DANTES	48	3	L	a,n	Yes
Art History	AP	3	6	L	a,n	Yes
Art History I	TECEP	60	3	L	a,n	Yes
Art History II	TECEP	60	3	L	a,n	Yes
Art/Studio Drawing or General Portfolio	AP	3	6	L	a	Yes
BIOLOGY						
Anatomy and Physiology	ECE	C	6	L	s	Yes
Anatomy and Physiology	TECEP	120	6	L	s	Yes
Biology	GRE	40th %ile	24	L,U	s	Yes
Biology	AP	3	8	L	s	Yes
General Biology	CLEP	50	6	L	s	Yes
Kinesiology	TECEP	60	3	L	s	Yes
Microbiology	ECE	C	3	L	s	Yes
Pathophysiology	ECE	C	3	U	s	Yes
BUSINESS						
Business in Society	TECEP	60	3	U	d	Yes
Business Law	TECEP	55	3	L		
Business Law II	DSST/DANTES	44	3	U		
Business Mathematics	DSST/DANTES	48	3	L		
Business Policy	TECEP	60	3	U		
Statistics (Business)	COSC	52	6	L	q	3 cr.
Federal Income Taxation	TECEP	60	3	U		
Financial Accounting	CLEP	50	3	L		
Introduction to Business	DSST/DANTES	46	3	L		
Introductory Business Law	CLEP	50	3	L		
Principles of Financial Accounting	DSST/DANTES	47	3	L		
CHEMISTRY						
Chemistry	GRE	40th %ile	24	L,U	s	Yes
Chemistry	AP	3	8	L	s	Yes
General Chemistry	CLEP	50	6	L	s	Yes
COMMUNICATION						
Principles of Public Speaking	DSST/DANTES		3	L	o	Yes
Introduction to the History of Film	TECEP	60	3	L	a	Yes
Introduction to News Reporting	TECEP	65	3	L		Yes
Public Relations Thought & Practice	TECEP	60	3	L		Yes

Discipline	Test Programs	Minimum Req'd Score	Credits	Level	General Education	Liberal Arts
COMPUTER SCIENCE						
C Programming	TECEP	35	3	L		
Computer Science	GRE	40th %ile	24	L,U		Yes/9 cr.
Computer Science A	AP	3	3	L		
Computer Science AB	AP	3	6	L		
Database Management	TECEP	65	3	L		
Intro to Computer Information Systems	TECEP	70	3	L		
Introduction to Computing	DSST/DANTES	400	3	L		
Information Systems & Computer Applications	CLEP	50	3	L		
Management Information Systems	DSST/DANTES	400	3	L		
Operating Systems	TECEP	51	3	L		
BASIC	TECEP	60	3	L		
QBASIC	TECEP	60	3	L		
Word Processing Fundamentals	TECEP	65	3	L		
CRIMINAL JUSTICE						
Criminal Justice	DSST/DANTES	400	3	L	b	Yes
Introduction to Law Enforcement	DSST/DANTES	45	3	L		
EARLY CHILDHOOD EDUCATION/EDUCATION						
Intro to Early Childhood Education	COSC	47	3	L		
Foundations of Education	DSST/DANTES	46	3	L	b	Yes
Literacy Instruction in Elementary School	ECE	C	6	U		
Early Language & Literacy Development	COSC	54	3	L		
EARTH SCIENCE						
Astronomy	DSST/DANTES	48	3	L	s	Yes
Physical Geology	DSST/DANTES	46	3	L	s	Yes
Physical Geology	TECEP	55	3	L	s	Yes
ECONOMICS						
Economics/Macroeconomics	AP	3	3	L	b	Yes
Economics/Microeconomics	AP	3	3	L	b	Yes
Financial Institutions & Markets	TECEP	65	3	U	b	Yes
Money and Banking	DSST/DANTES	48	3	U	b	Yes
Principles of Macroeconomics	CLEP	50	3	L	b	Yes
Principles of Microeconomics	CLEP	50	3	L	b	Yes
ENGLISH						
American Literature	CLEP	50	6	L	a	Yes
Analyzing/Interpreting Literature	CLEP	50	6	L	a	Yes
College Writing	ECE	C	3	L	e	Yes
English Composition (Essay format)	ECE	C	6	L	e	Yes

Discipline	Test Programs	Minimum Req'd Score	Credits	Level	General Education	Liberal Arts
English Composition I	TECEP	70	3	L	e	Yes
English Composition II	TECEP	70	3	L	e	Yes
English Composition w/Essay*	CLEP	50	6	L	e	Yes
English/Language & Composition	AP	3	6	L	e	Yes
English/Literature & Composition	AP	3	6	L	e	Yes
English Literature	CLEP	50	6	L	e	Yes
Literature in English	GRE	40th %ile	18	L,U	a,n	Yes
Shakespeare I	TECEP	60	3	U	a,n	Yes
FINANCE						
International Finance	TECEP	60	3	U	g	
Personal Finance	DSST/DANTES	400	3	L		
Principles of Finance	DSST/DANTES	46	3	L		
Principles of Finance	TECEP	50	3	L		
FRENCH						
College French Language:						
Level I	CLEP	50	6	L	n	Yes
Level II	CLEP	62	6	L	n	Yes
French Language	AP	3	6	L	n	Yes
French Literature	AP	3	6	L	a,n	Yes
GEOGRAPHY						
Human/Cultural Geography	DSST/DANTES	48	3	L	b,g,n	Yes
GERMAN						
College German Language:						
Level I	CLEP	50	6	L	n	Yes
Level II	CLEP	63	6	L	n	Yes
German Language	AP	3	6	L	n	Yes
GERONTOLOGY						
Foundations of Gerontology	ECE	C	3	U	b	Yes
Social Gerontology	TECEP	60	3	U	b	Yes
HEALTH						
Alcohol Abuse: Fundamental Facts	TECEP	60	3	U		Yes
Community Health	TECEP	60	3	U		
Substance (Drug &Alcohol) Abuse	DSSE/DANTES	400	3	U		Yes
Here's to your Health	DSSE/DANTES	400	3	L		
Substance Abuse: Fundamental Facts	TECEP	60	3	U		Yes
HISTORY						
A History of the Vietnam War	DSST/DANTES	44	3	L	g,n	Yes
Civil War and Reconstruction	DSST/DANTES	47	3	U	u	Yes
History/European	AP	3	6	L	g,n	Yes
History of the United States I	CLEP	50	3	L	u	Yes

Discipline	Test Programs	Minimum Req'd Score	Credits	Level	General Education	Liberal Arts
History of the United States II	CLEP	50	3	L	u	Yes
History/United States	AP	3	6	L	u	Yes
Intro to the Modern Middle East	DSST/DANTES	47	3	L	g,n	Yes
Rise and Fall of the Soviet Union	DSST/DANTES	45	3	U	g,n	Yes
Western Civilization I	CLEP	50	3	L	n	Yes
Western Civilization II	CLEP	50	3	L	n	Yes
Western Europe Since 1945	DSST/DANTES	45	3	L	g,n	Yes

HUMANITIES

Discipline	Test Programs	Minimum Req'd Score	Credits	Level	General Education	Liberal Arts
Humanities	CLEP	50	6	L	a,n	Yes
Introduction to the Art of the Theater	TECEP	60	3	L	a	Yes

HUMAN SERVICES

Discipline	Test Programs	Minimum Req'd Score	Credits	Level	General Education	Liberal Arts
Counselor Training Short-Term Client Systems	TECEP	60	3	U		
Introduction to Human Services	TECEP	60	3	L		

LATIN

Discipline	Test Programs	Minimum Req'd Score	Credits	Level	General Education	Liberal Arts
Latin/Latin Literature	AP	3	6	L	n	Yes
Latin/Virgil	AP	3	6	L	n	Yes

MANAGEMENT

Discipline	Test Programs	Minimum Req'd Score	Credits	Level	General Education	Liberal Arts
Advanced Labor Relations and Collective Bargaining	TECEP	50	3	U		
Human Resource Management	ECE	C	3	U		
Human Resource Management	DSST/DANTES	46	3	L		
Human Resource Management	TECEP	60	3	U		
Labor Relations	ECE	C	3	U		
Labor Relations and Collective Bargaining	TECEP	35	3	U		
Operations Management	TECEP	60	3	U		
Organizational Behavior	DSST/DANTES	48	3	L	b	Yes
Organizational Behavior	ECE	C	3	U	b	Yes
Organizational Behavior	TECEP	60	3	U	b	Yes
Principles of Management	CLEP	50	3	L		
Principles of Management	TECEP	60	3	L		
Principles of Supervision	DSST/DANTES	46	3	L		

MARKETING

Discipline	Test Programs	Minimum Req'd Score	Credits	Level	General Education	Liberal Arts
Advertising	TECEP	60	3	U		
Introduction to Marketing	TECEP	60	3	L		
Marketing Channels	TECEP	60	3	U		
Marketing Communications	TECEP	60	3	U		
Marketing Management Strategy	TECEP	50	3	U		
Marketing Research	TECEP	60	3	U		
Sales Management	CLEP	50	3	L		
Principles of Marketing	TECEP	70	3	U		

Discipline	Test Programs	Minimum Req'd Score	Credits	Level	General Education	Liberal Arts
MATHEMATICS						
Calculus	CLEP	50	3	L	q	Yes
Calculus AB	AP	3	3	L	q	Yes
Calculus BC	AP	3	6	L	q	Yes
College Algebra	CLEP	50	3	L	q	Yes
College Mathematics	CLEP	50	6	L	q	Yes
Fundamentals of College Algebra	DSST/DANTES	400	3	L	q	Yes
Mathematics	GRE	40th %ile	24	L,U	q	Yes
Pre-Calculus	CLEP	50	3	L	q	Yes
Principles of Statistics	DSST/DANTES	400	3	L	q	Yes
Principles of Statistics	TECEP	55	3	L	q	Yes
Statistics	AP	3	3	L	q	Yes
Statistics	ECE	C	3	L	q	Yes
MUSIC						
Music Theory	AP	3	6	L	a	Yes
NURSING						
Adult Nursing	ECE	C	8	U		
Community Focused Nursing	ECE	C	4	U		
Essentials of Nursing Care: Chronicity	ECE	C	3	L		
Essentials of Nursing Care: Health Diff.	ECE	C	3	L		
Essentials of Nursing Care: Health Safety	ECE	C	3	L		
Essentials Nursing Care: Reproductive Hlth	ECE	C	3	L		
Fundamentals of Nursing	ECE	C	8	L		
Health Differences Across The Life Span 1	ECE	C	3	L		
Health Differences Across The Life Span 2	ECE	C	3	L		
Health Differences Across The Life Span 3	ECE	C	3	L		
Management in Nursing	ECE	C	3	U		Yes
Maternal & Child Nursing (Associate)	ECE	C	6	L		
Maternal & Child Nursing (Baccalaureate)	ECE	C	8	U		
Maternity Nursing	ECE	C	3	L		
Nursing Concepts I	ECE	C	4	L		
Nursing Concepts II	ECE	C	4	L		
Nursing Concepts III	ECE	C	4	L		
Nursing Concepts IV	ECE	C	4	L		
Nursing Concepts V	ECE	C	4	L		
Nursing Concepts VI	ECE	C	4	L		

Discipline	Test Programs	Minimum Req'd Score	Credits	Level	General Education	Liberal Arts
Nursing Concepts: Found Prof. Practice	ECE	C	4	L		
Psychiatric/Mental Health Nursing	ECE	C	8	U		
Research in Nursing	ECE	C	3	U		
Transition Registered Profess Nurse Role	ECE	C	3	L		
PHILOSOPHY						
Bio-Ethics: Philosophical Issues	ECE	C	3	U	d	Yes
Ethics in America	DSST/DANTES	400	3	L	d	Yes
Ethics: Theory & Practice	ECE	C	3	U	d	Yes
PHYSICS						
Physics	GRE	40th %ile	24	L,U	s	Yes
Physics I	TECEP	85	3	L	s	Yes
Physics II	TECEP	85	3	L	s	Yes
Physics B	AP	3	8	L	s	Yes
Physics C/Electricity & Magnetism	AP	3	4	L	s	Yes
Physics C/Mechanics	AP	3	4	L	s	Yes
POLITICAL SCIENCE						
American Government	CLEP	50	3	L	b,u	Yes
Government & Politics/Comparative	AP	3	3	L	b,g,n	Yes
Government & Politics/U.S.	AP	3	3	L	b,u	Yes
Introduction to Political Science	TECEP	60	3	L	u	Yes
PSYCHOLOGY						
Abnormal Psychology Research Methods in Psychology	ECE	C	3	U	b	Yes
Abnormal Psychology	TECEP	60	3	U	b	Yes
Behavior Modification Techniques in Counseling	TECEP	65	3	U	b	Yes
Child Developmental Psychology	COSC	46	3	L	b	Yes
Developmental Psychology	TECEP	60	3	L	b	Yes
Fundamental of Counseling	DSST/DANTES	45	3	L	b	Yes
Human Growth & Development	CLEP	50	3	L	b	Yes
Industrial Psychology	TECEP	60	3	U	b	Yes
Infant/Toddler Growth & Development	COSC	58	3	L	b	Yes
Intro Educational Psychology	CLEP	50	3	L	b	Yes
Introduction to Counseling	TECEP	60	3	L	b	Yes
Introduction to Social Psychology	TECEP	60	3	U	b	Yes
Introductory Psychology	CLEP	50	3	L	b	Yes
Lifespan Developmental Psychology	DSST/DANTES	46	3	L	b	Yes
Lifespan Developmental Psychology	ECE	C	3	L	b	Yes
Psychology	AP	3	3	L	b	Yes
Psychology	GRE	40th %ile	18	L,U	b	Yes

Discipline	Test Programs	Minimum Req'd Score	Credits	Level	General Education	Liberal Arts
Psychology of Adulthood and Aging	ECE	C	3	U	b	Yes
Psychology of Personality	TECEP	70	3	U	b	Yes
Psychology of Women	TECEP	60	3	U	b	Yes
Research in Experimental Psychology	TECEP	55	3	U	b	Yes
Research Methods in Psychology	ECE	C	3	U		
Social Psychology	ECE	C	3	U		Yes
Thanatology: An Understanding of Death & Dying	TECEP	60	3	U	b	Yes
RELIGION						
Introduction to World Religions	DSST/DANTES	400	3	L	g,n	Yes
Religions of the World (Essay format)	ECE	C	3	U	g,n	Yes
SCIENCE						
Environment and Humanity	DSST/DANTES	46	3	L	g,s	Yes
Environmental Science	AP	3	4	L	g,s	Yes
Natural Sciences	CLEP	50	6	L	s	Yes
Principles of Physical Science I	DSST/DANTES	47	3	L	s	Yes
The Science of Nutrition	TECEP	60	3	L	S	Yes
SOCIAL SCIENCES/HISTORY						
Social Sciences/History	CLEP	50	6	L	b,n	Yes
American Dream (Essay format)	ECE	C	6	U	u	Yes
Cultural Diversity	ECE	C	3	U	b	Yes
Introductory Sociology	CLEP	50	3	L	b	Yes
Juvenile Delinquency	ECE	C	3	U	b	Yes
Marriage & the Family	TECEP	60	3	L	b	Yes
World Conflicts since 1900	ECE	C	3	U	b,g,n	Yes
World Population	ECE	C	3	U	b,g,n	Yes
SPANISH						
College Spanish Language:						
Level I	CLEP	50	6	L	n	Yes
Level II	CLEP	63	6	L	n	Yes
Spanish Language	AP	3	6	L		Yes
Spanish Literature	AP	3	6	L	a,n	Yes
TECHNICAL WRITING						
Technical Writing	DSST/DANTES	46	3	L	e*	Yes
Technical Writing	TECEP	45	3	L	e*	Yes
* exam fulfills 2nd half of "e" requirement						

APPENDIX C: CHARTER OAK CAPSTONE EXPERIENCE COURSES

Students matriculating in Charter Oak State College after July 1, 2009 will be required to complete a three-credit capstone experience. Students will still be required to complete a concentration rationale, but will not have the academic autobiography requirement. Some details are provided below.

(Adapted from Charter Oak publications)

At Charter Oak State College each student is required to complete a capstone experience as the academic culmination of his or her concentration. The capstone synthesizes the prior coursework in the concentration and officially completes the concentration. The purposes of this capstone experience are to demonstrate that students have a clear understanding of their concentration, that they have mastered the content of their selected fields of study, and that they can synthesize and apply what they have learned.

The capstone experience courses require a project that fully demonstrates that the student has fulfilled the various outcomes of the concentration. These projects may take a variety of formats: a research paper, scholarly essay, portfolio, creative work, presentation, business plan, case study, or other project appropriate to the concentration and to the student's competencies and interests.

For students who have selected the Liberal Studies or Individualized Studies concentration, the capstone experience is composed of two distinct but connected courses. 498, the one-credit course, forms the gateway to the two-credit capstone experience project, 499. Both 498 and 499 are offered, back to back, within a fifteen week semester. 498 is a five week course. 499 is a ten week course. In 498, the student formulates the project he/she is going to do to demonstrate their knowledge. In 499, the student carries out the project.

For students who have selected a Subject Area concentration, there is a three credit course requirement that will either be offered as an online course or as an individual contract.

APPENDIX D: EXAM LIST FOR EXCELSIOR COLLEGE

The following list is taken from the handbook, A Student Guide to Credit by Examination at Excelsior College, which is available at www.excelsior.edu. It outlines some exams that satisfy general education requirements. Use it only as a guide, as the handbook cautions, *"some degree programs have their own specific variation on fulfillment of general education requirements."*

Humanities Requirement

LOWER LEVEL
ECE - Introduction to Music
CLEP - American Literature
CLEP - Analyzing and Interpreting Literature
CLEP - French Language
CLEP - German Language
CLEP - Spanish Language
CLEP - English Literature
CLEP - Humanities (General)
DANTES - Art of the Western World
DANTES - Ethics in America
DANTES - Principles of Public Speaking
DANTES - Technical Writing
DANTES - Introduction to World Religions

UPPER LEVEL
ECE - American Dream
ECE - Bioethics: Philosophical Issues
ECE - Ethics: Theory & Practice
ECE - Religions of the World

Social Science/History Requirement

LOWER LEVEL

ECE - Life Span Developmental Psychology

CLEP - American Government

CLEP - Introduction to Educational Psychology

CLEP - History of the United States I and II

CLEP - Human Growth and Development

CLEP - Principles of Macroeconomics

CLEP - Principles of Microeconomics

CLEP - Introductory Psychology

CLEP - Social Sciences and History (General)

CLEP - Introductory Sociology

CLEP - Western Civilization I and II

DANTES - Fundamentals of Counseling

DANTES - General Anthropology

DANTES - Western Europe since 1945

DANTES - Criminal Justice

DANTES - Foundations of Educations

DANTES - Human/Cultural Geography

DANTES - Life Span Developmental Psychology

DANTES - Introduction to the Modern Middle East

DANTES - Organizational Behaviour

DANTES - History of the Vietnam War

Social Science/History Requirement

UPPER LEVEL

ECE - Abnormal Psychology

ECE - American Dream

ECE - Cultural Diversity

ECE - Foundations of Gerontology

ECE - Juvenile Deliquency

ECE - Organizational Behaviour

ECE - Psychology of Adulthood & Aging

ECE - Research Methods in Psychology

ECE - Social Psychology

ECE - World Conflicts since 1900

ECE - World Population

DANTES - Civil War and Reconstruction

DANTES - Money and Banking

DANTES - Rise and Fall of the Soviet Union

Written English Requirement (WER)

ECE - English Composition

Natural Sciences/Mathematics Requirement

LOWER LEVEL

ECE - Anatomy & Psysiology

ECE - Earth Science

ECE - Microbiology

CLEP - Biology

CLEP - Calculus (Q)

CLEP - Chemistry

CLEP - College Algebra (Q)

CLEP - College Mathematics (general) (Q)

CLEP - Natural Science (general)

CLEP - Precalculus (Q)

DANTES - Astronomy

DANTES - Fundamentals of College Algebra (Q)

DANTES - Environment and Humanity

DANTES - Physical Geology

DANTES - Principles of Physical Science

DANTES - Principles of Statistics (Q)

UPPER LEVEL

ECE - Pathophysiology

(Note: Q indicates that the exam fulfills the quantitative requirement included in some degree programs.)

APPENDIX E: ACCREDITING AGENCIES

National or Specialized Accrediting Agencies

Listed below are some of the agencies that are recognized.

Association of Advanced Rabbinical and Talmudic Schools,
Accreditation Commission

11 Broadway, Suite 405

New York, New York 10004

Tel. (212)363-1991, Fax (212) 533-5335

Distance Education and Training Council,
Accrediting Commission

1601 18th Street, NW

Washington, DC 20009

Tel. (202) 234-5100, Fax (202) 332-1386

E-mail address: Detc@detc.org

Web address:www.detc.org

New York State Board of Regents,
and the Commissioner of Education

State Education Department

The University of the State of New York

Albany, New York 12234

Tel. (518) 474-5844 Fax (518) 473-4909

E-Mail address: rmills@mail.nysed.gov

Web address: www.nysed.gov

Regional Accrediting Agencies

Listed below are the six regional accrediting agencies. Be aware that some of these agencies have commissions that also accredit vocational and non-degree granting institutions.

Middle States Association of Colleges and Schools,

Commission on Higher Education

Delaware, the District of Columbia, Maryland, New Jersey, New York, Pennsylvania, Puerto Rico, and the U.S. Virgin Islands.

3624 Market Street

Philadelphia, Pennsylvania 19104

Tel. (267) 284-5000, Fax (215) 662-5950

E-mail address: info@msche.org

Web address: www.msche.org

New England Association of Schools and Colleges,

Commission on Institutions of Higher Education

Connecticut, Maine, Massachusetts, New Hampshire, Rhode Island, and Vermont.

209 Burlington Road

Bedford, Massachusetts 01730-1433

Tel. (781) 271-0022, Fax (781) 271-0950

E-mail address: bbrittingham@neasc.org

Web address: www.neasc.org

North Central Association of Colleges and Schools,

The Higher Learning Commission

Arizona, Arkansas, Colorado, Illinois, Indiana, Iowa, Kansas, Michigan, Minnesota, Missouri, Nebraska, New Mexico, North Dakota, Ohio, Oklahoma, South Dakota, West Virginia, Wisconsin, and Wyoming.

30 North LaSalle Street, Suite 2400

Chicago, Illinois 60602

Tel. (312) 263-0456, (800) 621-7440, Fax (312) 263-7462

E-mail address: smanning@hlcommission.org

Web address: www.ncahigherlearningcommission.org

Northwest Commission on Colleges and Universities

Alaska, Idaho, Montana, Nevada, Oregon, Utah, and Washington.

8060 165th Avenue, NE, Suite 100

Redmond, Washington 98052

Tel. (425) 558-4224, Fax (425) 376-0596

E-mail address: selman@nwccu.org

Web address: www.nwccu.org

Southern Association of Colleges and Schools,
Commission on Colleges

Alabama, Florida, Georgia, Kentucky, Louisiana, Mississippi, North Carolina, South Carolina, Tennessee, Texas, and Virginia.

1866 Southern Lane

Decatur, Georgia 30033-4097

Tel. (404) 679-4512, Fax (404) 679-4528

E-mail address: bwheelan@sacscoc.org

Web address: www.sacs.org

Western Association of Schools and Colleges,
Accrediting Commission for Community and Junior Colleges

Two-year, associate degree-granting institutions located in California, Hawaii, the United States territories of Guam and American Samoa, the Republic of Palau, the Federated States of Micronesia, the Commonwealth of the Northern Mariana Islands, and the Republic of the Marshall Islands.

10 Commercial Boulevard, Suite 204

Novato, California 94949

Tel. (415) 506-0234, Fax (415) 506-0238

E-mail address: accjc@accjc.org

Web address: www.wascweb.org

Western Association of Schools and Colleges,

Accrediting Commission for Senior Colleges and Universities

Senior colleges and universities in California, Hawaii, the United States territories
of Guam and American Samoa, the Republic of Palau, the Federated States
of Micronesia, the Commonwealth of the Northern Mariana Islands and the
Republic of the Marshall Islands.

985 Atlantic Avenue, Suite 100

Alameda, California 94501

Tel. (510) 748-9001, Fax (510) 748-9797

E-mail address: wascsr@wascsenior.org

Web address: www.wascweb.org

APPENDIX F: DISTANCE EDUCATION & TRAINING COUNCIL—DETC

As a student interested in pursuing studies through nontraditional means you should be informed about the Distance Education & Training Council. The bulk of this book focuses on introducing you to nontraditional education and guiding you toward a degree program at a regionally accredited college. However, as noted in the "Accreditation" section, in addition to the regional accreditors, there are also national accrediting bodies.

The Distance Education and Training Council has been the standard-setting agency for correspondence study and distance education institutions since it was established in 1926. Its purpose was, and still is today, *"to foster and preserve high quality, educationally sound and widely accepted distance education and independent learning institutions."* DETC accredited institutions offer a wide range of programs including high school diplomas, certificate programs and college degrees in many different fields.

DETC schools offer students the opportunity to take courses via correspondence study or online. Some schools offer courses that have specific semesters, while others allow students to start their studies at any time and move along at their own pace.

As noted in the Accreditation section:

"When selecting a college, be sure to check if the college is accredited and by whom. Make sure it is a legitimate accreditor, one that is recognized by the USDE, CHEA or both, and be sure that the type of accreditation will suit your purposes."

DETC is recognized by the USDE and CHEA. Many employers require job candidates to have a degree from an institution accredited by an accreditor (national or regional) recognized by the USDE or CHEA, while some require a degree from a regionally accredited college. If you plan to attend a regionally accredited graduate school, it's a good idea to check with the school to be sure they will accept a nationally accredited degree, as some will accept only regional accreditation. It's wise to be fully informed.

In order to help facilitate credit transfer to regionally accredited colleges several DETC accredited schools have had their courses reviewed by the American Council on Education (ACE). As noted in the section of Noncollegiate Courses and Exams, ACE credit recommendations are recognized by many colleges across the U.S.

Distance Education & Training Council
1601 18th Street, N.W., Suite 2
Washington, DC 20009
202-234-5100
Fax- 202-332-1286
detc@detc.org
www.detc.org

APPENDIX G: EMPIRE STATE COLLEGE

Empire State College is another option for students who wish to pursue a degree through nontraditional means. At Empire State College you have much of the same flexibility, in terms of using credit by exam, traditional courses, online courses or prior learning assessment, as some of the other colleges discussed in this guide. However, you must earn at least 24 credits from the college for an associates degree or 32 credits for a bachelor's degree.

About Empire State College

Empire State College was founded in 1971 and is part of the State University of New York. The college is designed to serve adults pursuing associate, bachelor's and master's degrees. The college offers affordable, SUNY degrees onsite at 35 locations in New York state and abroad, as well as entirely online. With Empire State you choose how, when and where you will study. When you take courses at Empire State College, you are among the 17,600 adult learners served annually by the college.

Highlights include:

- Affordable SUNY tuition
- Degrees that can be tailored to meet your education, career and personal goals
- A clear process for assessing and awarding credit for college-level learning An independent study program, guided by outstanding SUNY faculty mentors, that allows you to study at your convenience
- "Transfer- friendly" policies
- Student online library and study resources

Regional Centers—Onsite

If you prefer to study near your home or office, you may enroll with one of 35 locations across New York State. You'll be able to combine working directly with a faculty mentor for one-to-one study; taking online courses; or participating in small study groups, seminars and residencies. Additionally, you'll have access to our wide array of student services and resources.

Center for Distance Learning—Online

With Empire State College's Center for Distance Learning (CDL), you can take a few courses or earn your entire degree online. Busy, working adults are increasingly turning to the web for quality education that fits into their lives. Whether you're on the road or prefer to study from the comfort of your home, the Center for Distance Learning offers you the chance to reach your goals. Students communicate with faculty and course instructors by means of e-mail, telephone and through discussion areas online.

When selecting a regional center consider the Hudson Valley Center. The center has a location in New City, which is right near Monsey. Feedback from students about the center is very positive. Students emphasized their appreciation for the center's staff and mentors for understanding their busy home and work life and helping them find the proper balance while pursuing their education.

Whether you want to study close to home, near your office, or somewhere in between, the Hudson Valley Center has four convenient locations. The College's faculty and

Empire State College has a minimum credit requirement. Students must earn at least 24 credits from the college for an associates degree or 32 credits for a bachelor's degree. These credits can be earned at a distance through online courses or guided independent study.

Empire State College has centers throughout the state. Enrolling at a regional center location does not mean you'll be attending traditional classroom classes. Students meet with a mentor when and as often as needed. The degree planning process and course study can also be done at a distance, by mail, email, fax and phone.

staff are dedicated to providing a combination of in person, group study, and online courses to suit your learning style and earn your degree. The Center's locations throughout the scenic Hudson Valley serves students from the Bronx, Westchester, Putnam, Rockland, Dutchess, Orange, Sullivan and Ulster Counties.

After enrolling at Empire State College students are assigned a mentor who will help plan your educational studies. Part of this planning process includes prior learning assessment where you can prepare the documentation to demonstrate the knowledge gained in yeshiva, seminary or from self-study. Students can also earn additional credits in Judaic studies guided independent study.

If you are not a New York State resident, consider the college's Center for Distance Learning (CDL). Students enrolling at the CDL pay in-state tuition regardless of where they live.

Empire State College

240 North Main Street

New City, NY 10956-5302

Phone: 845 708-7010 and 7011

Fax: 845 708-7013

Information for this section was adapted from www.ESC.edu and ESC publications.

APPENDIX H: THOMAS EDISON STATE COLLEGE

Another college for the nontraditional student to consider is Thomas Edison Sate College. The College also administers the TECEP exams and offers certificate programs which were discussed in previous sections.

Established over thirty years ago, Thomas Edison State College is one of the oldest schools in the country designed specifically for adults. The College provides flexible, collegiate learning opportunities for self-directed adults and offers **degree and certificate programs** in more than **100 areas of study.**

Thomas Edison State College offers a range of credit earning options for adult learners. Undergraduate students earn credit through a variety of programs that are all designed around the unique needs of adults. These options include:

- Transferring credits
- Credit for college-level knowledge acquired outside the classroom
- Online courses
- e-Pack® courses
- Guided Study courses
- Professional licenses and certifications
- Professional training programs
- Thomas Edison State College Examination Program (TECEP®)
- College Level Examination Program (CLEP)
- Defense Activity for Non-Traditional Educational Support (DANTES) Subject Standardized Tests
- New York University Foreign Language Proficiency Testing Program
- Excelsior College Examinations (ECE)
- Advanced Placement Program (AP)

Thomas Edison State College
101 West State Street

Trenton, NJ 08608

Tel: 888-442-8372

info@tesc.edu

www.tesc.edu

The information in this section is quoted or adapted from the Thomas Edison State College website or publications.

Bachelor of Arts

The Bachelor of Arts (BA) degree enables the student to develop a broad general knowledge of the traditional liberal arts disciplines, while providing the opportunity to develop a greater depth of knowledge in particular areas of study of interest to the student. This flexibility prepares students for career change or advancement, graduate education and provides personal enrichment.

Credit requirements are distributed among the traditional liberal arts areas (i.e., humanities, social sciences, natural sciences/mathematics) and free electives. Students have the opportunity either to pursue a concentration, choosing from subjects within one of the liberal arts areas; or to select one of the individual subject areas of study that provide for sequential course work in one particular subject of interest; or to select liberal studies, choosing from two or more disciplines within general education subject areas.

Courses transferred to Thomas Edison State College are equated to the following levels: 100, 200, 300 or 400. A maximum of two college-level courses equating to 100 level numbers may be applied toward the area of concentration, area of study or liberal studies area. A deeper knowledge of some

---

Credit Distribution Requirements

I. General Education	**60**
A. English Composition	6
B. Humanities	12
Must include at least two subject areas	
C. Social Sciences	12
Must include at least two subject areas	
D. Natural Sciences and Mathematics	12
Mathematics	(3)
Computer science course recommended	(3)
Other natural sciences/ mathematics	(6)
Must include at least two subject areas	
E. General Education Electives	18

II. Area Concentration, Area Of Study Or Liberal Studies Area — **33**

Must include at least two subject areas

A. English Composition

The area concentration includes 33 credits which must be chosen from humanities, or social or natural sciences/mathematics. The concentration includes at least three subject areas. Twelve credits must be earned in one subject area. A maximum of 18 credits may be earned in any one subject in order to have a balanced, interdisciplinary concentration.

Or

B. Area of Study

The area of study includes 33 credits in one subject area.

Or

C. Liberal Studies Area

The liberal studies area includes 33 credits, which include two or more liberal arts subject areas. For example, the area of study may include humanities, natural sciences and social sciences courses.

III. Free Electives	**27**
TOTAL	**120**

subjects is provided by requiring the remaining area of concentration, area of study or liberal studies area of study college-level courses be taken at levels 200, 300 or 400.

Keep the following notes in mind: Limitation of Credits in One Subject Area

No more than 70 credits earned in one subject area (e.g., art, music, journalism) will be counted toward meeting the degree requirements of the BA degree. Therefore, if you have credits in Bible, Talmud, and Jewish Law, and all are classified as religious studies, you will only be able to transfer a total of 70 credits in this subject area.

Junior College Limit

The College will accept a maximum of 80 junior or community college credits toward a bachelor's degree. The College will accept an unlimited number of credits in transfer from four-year institutions. So it is possible to transfer in an entire degree without taking any courses from TESC to complete your degree.

The College also discourages "self-advising." It makes good sense to have all credits pre-approved by Advisement at the College before the student registers for a particular course, to ensure that the potential credits will apply to the degree.

APPENDIX I: CONTACTS & RESOURCES

Colleges

The following 3 colleges have no residency requirement.

Charter Oak State College

55 Paul J. Manafort Drive

New Britain, CT

Tel: 860-832-8300

info@charteroak.edu

www.charteroak.edu

Excelsior College

7 Columbia Circle

Albany, NY 12203

Tel: 518-464-8500, Tel: 888-647-2388

admissions@excelsior.edu

www.excelsior.edu

Thomas Edison State College

101 West State Street

Trenton, NJ 08608

Tel: 888-442-8372

info@tesc.edu

www.tesc.edu

Empire State College has a residency requirement, in the sense that students must earn at least 30 credits from the college. These credits can be earned entirely at a distance.

Empire State College

2 Union Avenue

Saratoga Springs, NY 12886

Tel: 518-587-2100, Tel: 800-847-3000

admissions@esc.edu

www.esc.edu

Correspondence/Independent Study Courses

The following schools are regionally accredited and offer print-based courses. Some of these colleges also offer online self paced courses and some offer online semester based courses as well; however, semester based curses may be offered by another division of the college.

Indiana University
School of Continuing Studies
790 E. Kirkwood Avenue
Bloomington, Indiana 47405-7101
Tel: 800-334-1011, Tel: 812-855-2292
Fax: 812-855-8680
scs@indiana.edu
http://scs.indiana.edu

Louisiana State University
Independent & Distance Learning
1225 Pleasant Hall
Baton Rouge, LA 70803
Tel: 225-578-3920, Tel: 800-234-5046
Fax: 225-578-3090
iservices@outreach.lsu.edu
www.is.lsu.edu

Ohio University
Haning Hall
Athens, Ohio 45701
Tel: 800-444-2910
www.ohiou.edu/independent

Portland State University
Independent Study
PO Box 1491
Portland, OR 97207-14911
Tel: 503-725-4865, Tel: 800-547-8887 ext 4865
Fax: 503-725-4880
www.istudy.pdx.edu/

Sam Houston State University
Correspondence Course Division
Box 2536
Huntsville, Texas 77341-2536
Tel: 936-294-3909
cor_sav@shsu.edu
www.shsu.edu/~cor_www/

Texas Tech University
Outreach & Distance Education
9th & Indiana Ave
Lubbock, TX 79409-2191
Tel: 806-742-7200, Tel: 800-692-6877
http://www.depts.ttu.edu/ode/

University of Florida
2209 NW 13th St., Suite D
Gainesville FL 32609
Tel: 352- 392-1711, Tel: 800-327-4218
Fax: 352-392-6950
learn@dce.ufl.edu
www.correspondencestudy.ufl.edu

University of Idaho
Independent Study in Idaho
PO Box 443225
Moscow ID 83844-3225
Tel: 877-464-3246, Tel: 208-885-6641
Fax: 208-885-5738
indepst@uidaho.edu
www.uidaho.edu/isi

University of Missouri
Center for Distance and Independent Study
136 Clark Hall
Columbia, MO 65211-4200
Tel: 800-609-3727, Tel: 573-882-2491
cdis@missouri.edu
www.cdis.missouri.edu

University of North Dakota
Department of Correspondence & Online Studies
Division of Continuing Education
Gustafson Hall Room 103
3264 Campus Road Stop 9021
Grand Forks, ND 58202-9021
Tel: 701-777-2661, Tel: 800-342-8230
correspondence@mail.und.nodak.edu
www.conted.und.edu/correspondence

University of Wyoming
Outreach Credit Programs
Dept. 3274
1000 E. University Ave., 340 Wyo Hall
Laramie, WY 82071
Tel: 800-448-7801
uwcorr@uwyo.edu
http://outreach.uwyo.edu/correspondence

Examination Programs

Write, call, or search each programs' respective websites to learn more about the exams they offer.

ACTFL

The American Council on the Teaching of Foreign Languages offers oral proficiency tests in many languages, including Hebrew. The testing program is administered by Language Testing International.

Language Testing International
6 Executive Plaza, Suite 100
Yonkers, NY 10701
Tell: 1-800-486-8444, Tel: (914) 963-7110
Fax: (914) 963-7113
testing@languagetesting.com
www.languagetesting.com

AP Services
P.O. Box 6671
Princeton, NJ 08541-6671
Tel: 609-771-7300, Tel: 888-225-5427
apexams@info.collegeboard.org
www.collegeboard.org/ap

CLEP
P.O. Box 6600
Princeton, NJ 08541-6600
Tel: (800) 257-9558, Fax: (609) 771-7088
clep@info.collegeboard.org
www.collegeboard.org

Graduate Record Examinations®
GRE-ETS
P.O. Box 6000
Princeton, NJ 08541-6000

Tel: 609-771-7670, Tel: 866-473-4373

www.ets.org/gre

DANTES/DSST

Prometric

The DSST Program

2000 Lenox Drive, Third Floor

Lawrenceville, NJ 08648

Tel: 609-895-5011, Tel: 877-471-9860

Fax: 609-895-5026

pnj-dsst@prometric.com

www.getcollegecredit.com

NYU Language Exams

Center for Foreign Languages and Translation

10 Astor Place, Room 505

New York, NY 10003-7145

Tel: 212-998-7030

scps.foreignlanguages@nyu.edu

www.scps.nyu.edu/trans

Ohio University Course Credit by Exam

Haning Hall

Ohio University

Athens, Ohio 45701

800-444-2910

http://www.ohiou.edu/independent/ccewords.htm

TECEP

Thomas Edison State College

101 W. State Street

Trenton, NJ 08608

888-442-8372

info@tesc.edu

www.tesc.edu

Exam Study Guides

Barron's

Barron's publishes a series called EZ 101 Study Keys. While not geared to the CLEP or other exam programs, students find these inexpensive study guides helpful for preparing select exams. Barron's also publishes study guides for the GRE subject exams and AP programs.

Barron's Educational Series, Inc.

250 Wireless Blvd

Hauppauge NY, 11788

Tel: 800-645-3476

Tel: 631-434-3723 fax

barrons@barronseduc.com

www.barronseduc.com

CLEP® Official Study Guide

Published by the College Board and available from the College Board or your local or online bookseller. This is the "Official CLEP Guide."
www.collegeboard.org

InstantCert Academy

Offers online practice exams to help you prepare for select CLEP, DSST, ECE, and TECEP exams. Students pay a monthly or six-month membership fee and have unlimited access to the question database and detailed answers.

InstantCert Academy

3434 Kildaire Farm Rd, Suite 135

Cary, NC 27511

Tel: 866-705-0266

www.instantcert.com

iStudySmart.com

Prepares students for select CLEP, DSST, ECE and TECEP exams. Uses a study guide and textbook approach. Study guides available in print, online or CD format.

Tel: 800-737-2222

www.istudysmart.com

Research & Education Association (REA)

Publishes study guides to help prepare students for the CLEP and other exam programs.

REA

61 Ethel Road West

Piscataway, New Jersey 08854

Tel: 732-819-8880

info@rea.com

www.rea.com

The Princeton Review

Publishes study guides for the GRE subject exams and AP exams.

The Princeton Review

2315 Broadway

New York, NY 10024

Tel: 212-874-8282

Fax: 212- 874-0775

www.PrincetonReview.com

APPENDIX J: COLLEGE: ISSUR CHEFTZA OR GAVRA?

A preliminary examination of the college question

We have all heard about the differing opinion regarding the permissibility of attending college. With the popularity of nontraditional education, specifically with the ability to earn a degree without attending a traditional college campus, we have to examine the issue more closely. What problems are associated with colleges: is it attending the college, an *issur cheftza*? Or is it more of an *issur gavra*, meaning that a person may not have a degree; since having the degree itself is the problem. Now that we got some of the basic definitions out of the way, we can apply it to the discussion at hand. How do we view distance learning, or earning a degree without attending a college campus? If the problem with college is an *issur cheftza*, if you can earn the degree without stepping foot on campus, there should be no question as to its permissibility. However, if you learn that the issue is an *issur gavra*, it should make no difference whether you earn the degree through on-campus attendance or via distance learning. The bottom line is that you earn a degree, and having the degree is the problem.

In the last few years, with the widespread use of the internet, even those who held the college issue is an *issur cheftza* had to reexamine the question. While it would seem that if one is earning his degree by distance learning he avoids the college campus and thus the *issur cheftza*, the creation of the virtual campus now adds a new dimension to the question. If one is taking online courses, how do we view a virtual campus? Would taking an online course through a virtual campus constitute an *issur cheftza*? Or perhaps a virtual campus by definition cannot be called a *cheftza* since there is no *mamashos*?

According to those who are of the opinion that the college issue is an issue of *issur gavra*, is it any college course that would be assur, or must we examine the content of each individual course? Or does the mere fact that it is a college course or degree cause the *issur gavra* to manifest itself?

It is my belief that in essence there is an agreement among all the opinions. Everyone agrees there is both an issue of *issur cheftza* and *gavra*. In truth, each of the opinions are only addressing parts of the general college issue. Those who rule that there is an *issur cheftza* are primarily discussing the general culture that permeates many college campuses. In this case, the issue is not so much the fact that it is a college, but rather a place in which the atmosphere may run counter to Torah ideals and values. Those in the *issur cheftza* camp will agree that there is also an issue of *issur gavra,* and the content of the courses must be examined to ensure that the content and ideals are not antithetical to Torah thought. The fact that one may be taking courses off campus does not permit the study of heretical ideas. Similarly, those in the *issur gavra* camp also have concerns about what goes on the college campus. However, they are primarily addressing the education and focused on the courses.

Therefore, it is my humble opinion that we must be stringent and take into account the concerns addressed by all and proceed with caution. As with all *halachic* issues, the matter should be discussed with a competent *halachic* authority.

DA'AS COLLEGE

ABOUT THE AUTHOR

Reuven Frankel is the Dean of AHS Institute. He is also an instructor of Judaic Studies and Business, and a prior learning evaluator for regionally accredited colleges. In addition, he is consulted by *Rabbonim, Roshei Yeshiva,* and *Maggedei Shiur* to help counsel individuals on nontraditional college degree options and to establish college credit programs.

When Reuven Frankel discusses the college process, it's not just something that he read about in books or heard about from others. He went through the process, taking correspondence courses, CLEP exams, and online courses. As time went on, his interest in distance education grew and he began to develop and teach distance learning courses and now he shares this knowledge of nontraditional college degree options to help others like you.

If you would like to reach the author to comment, ask questions, or arrange for lectures, he can be contacted through the publisher at 845-510-3162 or **bochursguide@gmail.com**.

> **To order copies of this book for study groups or schools, or for customized versions of this book, please contact the publisher.**

www.ingramcontent.com/pod-product-compliance
Lightning Source LLC
Chambersburg PA
CBHW031249090426
42742CB00007B/383